From Victim

...ory

Also by Gary Schulz

The Discipling Father
Setting the Captives Free
New Wine New Wineskins
God's Creation of the Sexual Union
If You Love Me …
Partners
Saved from Our Enemies
Good News of Jesus Christ
Eternal Life What Is It?
God's Creation of Work
The Power of God's Grace
God's Creation, the Family
Marriage Enrichment
Passing Your Faith
Freedom from Anger
Clearly Seen
Creation to Rebellion to Restoration
Oil in Your Lamp
Wimps!
Controlling Parent Controlling Child
Restoring Broken Walls

From Victim to Victory

Gary Schulz

WESTBOW
PRESS
A DIVISION OF THOMAS NELSON

WestBow Press books may be ordered through booksellers or by contacting:

WestBow Press
A Division of Thomas Nelson
1663 Liberty Drive
Bloomington, IN 47403
www.westbowpress.com
1-(866) 928-1240

Because of the dynamic nature of the Internet, any web addresses or links contained in this book may have changed since publication and may no longer be valid. The views expressed in this work are solely those of the author and do not necessarily reflect the views of the publisher, and the publisher hereby disclaims any responsibility for them.

Any people depicted in stock imagery provided by Thinkstock are models, and such images are being used for illustrative purposes only.

Certain stock imagery © Thinkstock.

ISBN: 978-1-4497-7040-2 (sc)
ISBN: 978-1-4497-7039-6 (e)
ISBN: 978-1-4497-7041-9 (hc)

Library of Congress Control Number: 2012921219

Printed in the United States of America

WestBow Press rev. date: 11/26/2012

Kingdom Come Publications
81 Oaklawn Dr.
Midland, MI 48640

www.kingdomcomepublications.com

Contents

Chapter 1

What Is a Victim?

Those of us who have children have all seen a two-year-old throw a temper tantrum. Something doesn't go his way, he doesn't get what he wants, or he doesn't want to do what he is told, so he bursts into tears, falls down on the floor, and kicks and screams. All this flailing and carrying on is to get everyone's attention. His antics are making a strong declaration: "I am hurt. Everyone should come to my aid and give me what I want [demand]." He portrays himself as the victim, and he uses his role to manipulate others so that they will give in to his will. [The child could be male or female, but for ease of reference, we have referred to the child as male in the singular context.]

No one had to teach this child how to manipulate through a temper tantrum. He acquired this ability at conception. It is part of his innate nature, like an instinct. King David understood. He wrote, "Look, I was guilty of sin from birth, a sinner the moment my mother conceived me." Psalm 51:5 (NET)

This little child knows that his behavior is only an act of defiance for the purpose of getting his way. If everyone leaves the house so that his screaming cannot be heard and his flailing cannot be seen, he immediately stops.

I remember when I was a kid, about five years old, when my mother sent me to my upstairs bedroom because I had disobeyed. There was a door at the bottom of the stairs, which my mother had shut. I remember hanging over the railing so that my loud cries of defiance could be heard. I kept it up for some time, because I could hear my mother working around the house near the stairway door. But she just let me cry and gave no response. Then I heard the vacuum cleaner running and knew that it would drown out my screaming. Now there was no chance for her to hear me, so I just gave up in defeat. I don't remember throwing a tantrum after that incident. The point: I knew exactly what I was doing. I was portraying myself as the victim, and I was demanding attention. Even though I was being punished for violating my mother's demands, I attempted to turn the whole episode around so that I became the victim and my mother the perpetrator.

A Temper-Tantrum Society

Our society is being consumed by victimization. I don't mean that we are increasingly under attack by perpetrators (although that is also true). I mean that we have a culture that creates victims. Some people may have been under attack and consequentially have legitimately become victims. For example, the woman who is raped is certainly a victim of that rape. No one should want to become a victim. However, we have a society that thrives on defining oneself as a victim. Becoming a victim in the eyes of others warrants special powers, attention, privileges, entitlements, and sympathy. Victims can demand special privileges that others do not have. Victims can exhibit certain objectionable behaviors without being rejected.

A two-year-old who throws a temper tantrum in order to get his or her way needs swift discipline from Dad or Mom so that the child knows those tactics don't work. However, how often have you seen a child at the checkout counter with his or her mom reach for the candy? Mom says no, so the child begins the victim act. The child becomes very dramatic and loud so as to draw everyone's attention and embarrass the mother. If she gives in, she will be rewarding this behavior, and it will happen again. If she disciplines her child right there in the store, she subjects herself to the judgment of those around her. If she spanks her son or daughter for rebelling against her authority, she could be accused of child abuse. The child's behavior is the strength for getting his or her way, and our culture supports the rebellion.

Our intolerance for child discipline has gone on for decades now.

These two-year-olds have become teenagers and adults. Teenage behavior in the classroom is filled with filthy language, inattention, disobedience, disruption, and so on. Teachers are frustrated by the lack of respect and obedience in the classroom. Many have left the teaching profession because it is just too stressful to deal with the lack of order, obedience, respect, and decency.

When I was a child, my dad told me that if I got a spanking from the teacher at school, he would give me another one at home. If I had talked the way some students mouth off to teachers today, I would have had my mouth washed out with a bar of soap. Today, if a teacher lays a hand on a student, his or her father may file a lawsuit, there may be a charge of child abuse by the authorities, and the teacher may lose his or her job. All this is to the detriment of the student and society. The student's misbehavior will continue, and he or she will likely live as an adult, proclaiming victimization. It worked to get his or her way at age two, when a teen, and now as an adult.

Professionals and politicians are struggling with our declining academics in American schools. We have blamed the problem on ineffective teachers. I never hear that—just maybe—the child is the main problem. We throw more and more money into the school system to no avail. Teachers are blamed for the problem, and our leaders have fallen to the victim's tactics. The temper tantrum worked. Someone else is to blame, not the poor, defenseless child.

What Is a Victim?

We normally think of a victim as an unfortunate person who deserves attention, mercy, understanding, compassion, and aid. It is assumed that our sacrificial attention should go to the victim.

The dictionary defines a victim as

1. An unfortunate person who suffers from some adverse circumstance[1]
2. A person who is tricked or swindled[1]
3. A living being sacrificed to some deity, or in the performance of a religious rite; a creature immolated, or made an offering of[2]

---

1   WordNet 1.7 Copyright 2001 by Princeton University. All rights reserved.
2   *Webster's Revised Unabridged Dictionary*, Version published 1913 by the C. & G. Merriam Co. Springfield, Mass., under the direction of Noah Porter, DD, LLD. This version

4. A person or thing destroyed or sacrificed in the pursuit of an object, or in gratification of a passion; as, a victim to jealousy, lust, or ambition[2]
5. A person or living creature destroyed by, or suffering grievous injury from, another, from fortune or from accident; as, the victim of a defaulter; the victim of a railroad accident[2]
6. Hence, one who is duped, or cheated; a dupe; a gull[2]

These are clearly adverse circumstances, and the victimization was not by choice; it happened to individuals without their permission. However, many choose to become victims because of the manipulation that is possible. They may have been victims of serious abuse of one sort or another, but now they hold onto their identity as victims because of the privilege offered to them. The initial abuse was not a choice, but holding onto the identity as a victim is a choice.

It is a choice, but it may not be a cognitive choice. It may be just a response to the rewards given when classified as a victim. The two-year-old does not sit in his bedroom plotting his next temper tantrum. The child is not even aware of the intricacies of his or her manipulative behavior. It is just a spontaneous and natural reaction of defiance to a situation that portrays him or her as a victim. But it is still a willful choice.

Self-Victimization

In this study, we reveal many who are victims by choice, and we show that the true source of their victimization is not their circumstances, an organization, the government, or people. Their greatest source comes from believing lies about themselves, others, and situations. In short, they are victims of believing a lie and living out a lie. They may be rewarded for their victim identity, but in the end, they come up short. People with a victim mentality do not live victorious lives.

Certainly there are true victims. Someone may become crippled from a car accident. Someone may have been mugged or raped. Someone may have been abused as a child. Someone may have lost his or her job. Someone may have lost a house in a natural disaster. Someone may have a debilitating disease. The list of possibilities is endless. The issue is not about someone who has unwillingly become a victim. The issue is one of self-perception.

is copyrighted (C) 1996, 1998 by MICRA, Inc. of Plainfield, NJ. Last edit February 3, 1998.

Ironically, sometimes the greatest victimization is not what happens outwardly or physically or even emotionally. The greatest victimization occurs when the victims take on identities as victims. They see themselves as being victims. It is not so much an issue of what happened to them but rather who they are. Defining yourself as a victim is a choice to victimize yourself. It is a trap that promises special advantages but in reality creates a misguided bondage.

Adam and Eve, the First Self-Proclaiming Victims

Self-victimization began in the beginning, when Adam and Eve disobeyed God and ate of the Tree of the Knowledge of Good and Evil. It should have been obvious that they willfully failed to obey God's command and warning to them, but instead of confessing their guilt, they made themselves out as victims. They made excuses and blamed their behavior on others.

> Then the man and his wife heard the sound of the LORD God as he was walking in the garden in the cool of the day, and they hid from the LORD God among the trees of the garden.
> But the LORD God called to the man, "Where are you?"
> He answered, "I heard you in the garden, and I was afraid because I was naked; so I hid."
> And he said, "Who told you that you were naked? Have you eaten from the tree that I commanded you not to eat from?"
> The man said, "The woman you put here with me—she gave me some fruit from the tree, and I ate it."
> Then the LORD God said to the woman, "What is this you have done?"
> The woman said, "The serpent deceived me, and I ate." (Genesis 3:8–13 NIV)

Adam blamed God and the woman God gave him for his own choice to disobey. Eve blamed the serpent. Neither of them took personal responsibility for their disobedience. Instead, they made themselves a victim of others, placing the blame on someone else. Adam blamed God for setting him up with his wife, and Eve blamed the serpent. Notice that Eve made a choice to believe the serpent, which also meant that she chose to believe that God was lying to her about dying if she ate of the forbidden tree.

Somehow she saw herself as a victim of the serpent, but it was her choice to trust the serpent and distrust God.

Likewise, Adam knew what God told him about this dangerous tree. It was Adam's choice to follow his wife's lead rather than God's commands. He could have been victorious. He could have stepped in and told the serpent to leave.

Are we any different than Adam and Eve? Of course, we do not live in the garden of Eden. But have we not inherited a sinful nature from Adam and Eve. This nature is prone to blaming others for our shortcomings by making ourselves out to be a victim.

Blaming is the victim's tool for projecting the responsibility and guilt on others to relieve themselves from guilt. They portray themselves as a poor victim of someone's sin against them.

The Devil's Schemes

The Devil took advantage of the innocence and naivety of Adam and Eve. Remember, they had never witnessed good and evil before this time. They were responsible for their own behavior, but the Devil was right there to lie and to present temptation.

What would have happened if Adam and Eve had taken personal responsibility before God? What if they had not hidden from God, but sought God's mercy? What if they humbly came to God, trusting in his compassion and love, and confessed their disobedience? In essence, what if they had not portrayed themselves as the victims of others? Would God have had mercy on them?

Since that is not what happened, we cannot say what God would have done. But we do know that he sent Jesus so that our relationship with him could be reconciled and restored to its perfect state.

The Devil portrayed God as a selfish, deceitful liar who only wanted to keep Adam and Eve in bondage so that they would not become like God. Once Adam and Eve took the bait, they became the victims of distrust. It is one thing to distrust an evil person, but when man distrusts God's love, his commands, and his word, who can he trust from this point on? Once distrust in God takes root, we become victims of the Devil. Paul warned us to be aware of his schemes so that he would not outwit us. (2 Corinthians 2:11; Ephesians 6:10–12). And Peter compared him to a roaring lion that is roaming about, seeking someone to devour (1 Peter 5:8). David describes our enemy who lies in wait like a lion to capture his victim.

He lies in wait near the villages; from ambush he murders the innocent, watching in secret for his victims. He lies in wait like a lion in cover; he lies in wait to catch the helpless; he catches the helpless and drags them off in his net. His victims are crushed, they collapse; they fall under his strength. (Psalm 10:8–10 NIV)

This sly, patient, but deliberate enemy described in Psalms 10 could be an evil person who can be seen, but we have an enemy in this life that cannot be seen. The Devil delights in bringing situations into our lives that make us see ourselves as being a victim. Ironically, we are the Devil's victims, and he captures us by leading us into thinking we are victims. A victim is captive; he or she is not free. A victim may use the victim identity to manipulate others, but inwardly the person is not victorious. Victory comes from being set free from the label of "victim." The Devil seeks to devour us. He comes to steal, kill, and destroy (John 10:10). He comes to scheme against us in darkness, where we cannot see his ploys. Jesus called him the father of lies (John 8:44).

This study should make us wise to the Devil's schemes so that we do not become his victims. He knows that if we take on a self-image as being a victim of others, and even God, we will be trapped with no way out.

Reflection Questions

How have you portrayed yourself as a victim?

What do you complain about the most? How does your complaining define yourself as the victim?

Have your children succeeded in their temper tantrums? How has this affected their behavior now that they are older?

Where do you find yourself blaming? How is your blaming a cover-up or an excuse for your own behavior?

Chapter 2

Becoming a Victim

How does one become a victim? First, we must all realize that we are born with the tendency to be the center of attention as a result of our inherent sinful nature. The two-year-old did not have to be taught to play the victim role when he or she threw a temper tantrum. Parents must teach the child with loving discipline to refrain from these tantrums.

Some children have not been properly disciplined. And many children have been subject to abuse and have become true victims. When this happens, it is all the more likely that they will grow up with a victimized view of themselves and live out a victim role.

I have ministered the love and truth of God in prisons for many years. I have known men who have grown up in the most disadvantaged and hostile environments. I have heard powerful statements from dozens, if not hundreds of prisoners: "I thank God for coming to prison. If I were still on the streets, I would likely be dead by now from violence or drugs. It is here in prison that I found Jesus." Another comment I have heard numerous times: "Here I am in prison, and I have never been so free!"

There is no question that most prisoners have been victims of abusive and hostile environments in their formative years. There is no excuse for their criminal behavior, but I often wonder where I would be if I were subject to their circumstances. Many of these men grew up in broken, abusive homes. Some lived in environments where Mom and Dad never married. In fact, Dad may have had children with several mothers, none of them his wife. Typically, the son is primarily raised on the streets by his peers. The streets are filled with drugs and violence. This may have gone on for many generations, such that a normal, healthy family had not been seen. Anger and rage are an everyday occurrence. It is not uncommon for father and son to be in prison at the same time.

One does not have to be in prison to have grown up with an angry father or mother. The God-given family structure is rapidly disintegrating. Divorce affects most children today. The courts are quick to convict a father of child abuse, but they are also quick to issue a divorce, which is a devastating abuse to any child.

Sexual crimes are out of control. Most of these offenses are with teenagers or young children. Accurate sexual abuse statistics are difficult to acquire because much abuse goes unreported, but we do know that large segments of our population have been sexually abused.

Abuse Statistics

Those who have been true victims in their formative years are prone to see themselves as victims in their everyday circumstances and relationships, even when they are not the target of abuse. We live in a very abusive society, and, consequently, many more are taking on a victim identity.

According to the National Crime Victimization Survey, there were over 21,000 victimization crimes in 2008 to people twelve years or older. The victimization rate is 19.8 abuses for every 1,000 people. Obviously, not everyone has been criminally abused, and those who are abused could be abused multiple times. Once a significant abuse takes place in our lives, we can begin to see ourselves as a victim. The seeds of our identity as a victim can take root.

These results do not include those less than twelve years of age. The US Census Bureau, *Statistical Abstract of the United States: 2011* reported over 771,000 abuses to children from birth to eighteen years of age. These abuses include neglect, physical abuse, sexual abuse, emotional maltreatment, medical neglect, and others. The rate is 10.3 reported abuses for every 1,000 children eighteen or younger. Many of these children grow up seeing abuse to others and as victims of abuse throughout their childhood. They grow up with a view that victimization is normal—expect to be a victim—you are a victim. These formative years are much more critical than being victimized for the first time as an adult.

These are reported abuses. Many abuses go unreported, especially abuses within the family. In addition, there are serious emotional abuses that are not considered criminal, so they are not counted in these statistics. Anger, for example, is epidemic in our society. A child who is subjected to continual anger from a parent is most likely emotionally wounded. Every child is born with a need to be loved, encouraged, taught, lovingly disciplined, and cared for by his or her parents. An angry parent is a self-focused parent. The parent's internal needs become more important than the child's needs. Anger and angry words pour forth from the parent and create a rejected view in the child's mind and heart. The child's view of himself or herself is greatly determined by the parent's view as projected by the parent's attitudes, words, and behaviors. An angry parent can destroy a child's confidence, implying that he or she is not worth loving or will ever be loved. These wounds can grow very deep, and they may never heal.

We hear the saying, "Sticks and stones can break my bones, but names will never hurt me." This saying is a lie. In fact, bones will heal; a wounded heart may fester for a lifetime.

Addictive behaviors of parents are also not necessarily criminal but are most likely very abusive to all family members. For example, an alcoholic father or mother can cripple an entire family, creating childhood wounds and negative self-perceptions that may never go away. "One in five adult Americans has lived with an alcoholic relative while growing up. These children are in general at greater risk for having emotional problems than children whose parents are not alcoholics."[1]

Divorce is a very serious form of abuse on all family members, especially children. There is about one divorce for every two marriages. "Half of the children born this year to parents who are married will see their parents divorce before they turn 18."[2] Forty percent of children growing up in America today are being raised without their fathers.[3] The detrimental effects on child development are staggering.

There are other forms of abuse that increase the number of true victims in our society. Nearly everyone has been a victim of something or someone.

---

1   "American Academy of Child and Adolescent Psychiatry." *American Academy of Child and Adolescent Psychiatry.* No. 17.12/11 (2011): 3. Web. 24 Oct. 2012. <http://www. aacap.org/galleries/FactsForFamilies/17_children_of_alcoholics.pdf>

2   Fagen, Patrick F., and Robert Rector. "The Effects of Divorce on America." *The Heritage Foundation.* The Heritage Foundation, 05 2000. Web. 30 Oct 2012. <http://www. heritage.org/research/reports/2000/06/the-effects-of-divorce-on-america>.

3   Horn, Wade, and Andrew Bush. *Fathers, Marriage, and Welfare Reform.* Indianapolis: Hudson Institute, 1997. 35. Print.

Victims tend to propagate victims. For example, angry fathers will typically abuse their children in their anger. It may be physical, but more than likely, the abuse will be verbal. Rash words come from an angry person. A child looks to his or her father for love, worth, and encouragement. An angry father may use his words to degrade, reject, and discourage his children. When his son grows up, he, too, may become an angry father because of his own wounds, inflicted on him by his father. His inner wounds will consume his life, his view of himself, his behavior, and his thoughts. And he may destroy his relationships just like his dad. The cycle of anger can pass from generation to generation due to the wounds inflicted by the father on the very soul of his sons.

This generational cycle is common with many destructive behaviors. "Alcoholism runs in families, and children of alcoholics are four times more likely than other children to become alcoholics themselves."[4] Sin is generational. We sin because Adam and Eve sinned. They passed it on to their children, and eventually it was passed on to us. We are all victims of someone's sin. We are all sinners, because we all wound others.

Abuse Fosters a Victim Mentality

A victim is typically a wounded person. The wounds usually occurred during childhood. During this time, they were likely victims of physical abuse, abandonment, neglect, angry parent(s), sexual abuse, divorced parents, drug and alcohol abuse within the home, fatherless home, and so on. During these formative years, a child develops his or her views of life, family, God, and, in terms of victimization, of himself. He begins to see himself as a victim, and in these abusive circumstances, he is a victim. However, as the years proceed, he develops a picture of himself as a person who will always be a victim. He struggles with being loved, and he struggles with having a loving view of himself. All relationships and situations become a threat of being victimized. He does not trust anyone's love or motives.

This insecurity carries on into adult years. If he is to find security, he believes it has to come from himself. Even though he does not love himself, he is driven to strive for security. Physical security is important, but emotional security becomes most important. Physical security is usually

---

4   "American Academy of Child and Adolescent Psychiatry." *American Academy of Child and Adolescent Psychiatry.* No. 17.12/11 (2011): 3. Web. 24 Oct. 2012. <http://www.aacap.org/galleries/FactsForFamilies/17_children_of_alcoholics.pdf

easily obtained, although the one who has developed a victim mentality may never feel secure, no matter what the circumstances. He may even experience panic attacks and become afraid to leave his house.

Physical security can be established by physical means. One could carry a gun, move to a safer environment, become strong, and even become a martial arts expert. Many men with extreme anger and rage engage in many physical fights as a means of protecting themselves. Even though the fight is physical, the real battle is fear and insecurity within their own soul.

Emotional insecurity is not as easily remedied. Victims now see themselves as unloved, unlovable, and the target of everyone's offense. They feel rejected before anything has happened that would warrant rejection. Everyone becomes their enemy. Consequently, they become very accusatory and react defensively in most situations and relationships. If anything happens that is negative, it is viewed as a personal attack. They are victims by their own definition. Ironically, they become very offensive to those around them and welcome negative confrontations. The confrontations confirm their self-view of themselves as victims. They never see themselves as setting the stage for their own rejection.

A Victim Mentality Separates Us from God

Adam and Eve saw themselves as victims. They had two sons, Cain and Abel. Cain was a typical older brother. How many times have we seen the older brother who picks on his younger sibling? He is older and bigger, and he picks on his younger brother until his brother cries and gets angry. Then he turns the entire situation around, making himself the victim. His dad corrects him for picking on his brother, but the older brother just gets angry, blaming the entire episode on his younger brother.

I imagine that Adam and Eve struggled to raise Cain and Abel. And they did not have child-rearing advice books by James Dobson or Kevin Leman to read. They didn't even have other parents available for wisdom.

Cain and Abel grew up, but Cain's selfish childhood rivalry continued. They both brought sacrifices to offer to God (Genesis 4:1–16). Abel brought the best of his flock, and the Lord looked on his offering with favor. Cain brought some of his fruits and vegetables, and God was not pleased with his offering. Cain became angry and downcast, and God warned him about his selfish and uncontrolled anger.

> Then the LORD said to Cain, "Why are you angry? Why is your face downcast? If you do what is right, will you not be accepted? But if you do not do what is right, sin is crouching at your door; it desires to have you, but you must master it."
> (Genesis 4:6–7 NIV)

Cain pouted, became angry, and took on his victim role. Instead of taking personal responsibility for his own actions, he blamed his brother. He concluded that the only reason his offerings did not bring forth favor from the Lord was because Abel's sacrifice was better than his. Instead of repenting and bringing the best of his harvest, he went out and murdered his brother. Abel had done nothing directly offensive to Cain; he just offered his sacrifices to God out of his own love for and faith in God (Hebrews 11:4). Cain's offensive behavior was completely unfounded. Cain saw himself as a victim of Abel.

> Do not be like Cain, who belonged to the evil one and murdered his brother. And why did he murder him? Because his own actions were evil and his brother's were righteous. (1 John 3:12 NIV)

God warned Cain about his anger. He instructed him to conquer the sin that was crouching at the door of his soul (Genesis 4:7). But Cain, like his father, Adam, did not heed God's warning. He killed his brother, and God dealt with his sin. The Lord put a curse on the fruitfulness of his farming, and God also cast him from his presence.

Both Adam and Cain did not take personal responsibility for their actions. They both saw themselves as victims and blamed others. And both of them were cursed in their work, and both were cast from God's presence (Genesis 3:17–19, 23–24; 4:12–16).

We should take serious warning from these men's lives. If we portray ourselves as victims, we will have laid the groundwork for limiting the fruitfulness of our labor, and we will have distanced ourselves from the Lord's presence. The curse does not have to come as a direct one from God. Victims normally do not make good employees. Since they see themselves as victims, they may not strive to succeed. Their separation from God will be the result of identifying with a victim, rather than with our identity as children of God who are loved, protected, and provided for by the hand of God.

We should see from Adam and Cain that portraying ourselves as a victim does not require that we are true objects of victimization. It is very true that those who have a history of being true victims may identify themselves as victims and live the rest of their lives in the bondage of this victim identity. The Devil would like to see everyone walking around with a victim mentality. He can tempt us just by taking advantage of our sinful nature that is prone to blame, envy, anger, and selfish gain. If he can also subject us to episodes of real victimization abuse, all the better for setting us up for a lifetime of bondage.

The bondage is one of fear and insecurity. As time progresses, victims find they have a certain amount of security in their victimized view of themselves. If someone is a victim, then he is never responsible for rejection. The perpetrator is obviously the guilty, offending party. This allows the victim to condone any personal behavior. Everyone else is at fault, since others are the ones who are on the offense to victimize the victim. Even though this becomes the victim's security, it never satisfies, because the victim has isolated himself from any intimate relationships. The victim mentality says that no one can be trusted. Any act of love toward him is perceived as a deceptive plot to take advantage of him. He concludes that no one loves him. He is in a trap of his own making. It may have begun in his early years, when truly a victim. But now, as an adult, he is acting out his role as a victim, because he sees himself as an unloved person.

A victim sees himself as being sinned upon, so he thinks he is justified in feeling and acting the way he does. He does not see that he is in bondage, because he cannot forgive and love, and he does not know the love of God. Instead, he accuses and retaliates with his own sin.

Escape is found in seeing and believing the truth and then acting on it. Paul wrote, "be transformed by the renewing of you mind" (Romans 12:2). This is the first secret to deliverance. The second is to repent of this wayward view and behavior. A perpetual victim is not walking with God. Change requires submission to God and obedience to his commands. This will require the exact opposite behavior of a victim. These two behaviors—being a victim or being victorious as a loved child of God—are directly opposed to each other.

Reflection Questions

Have you been abused in your lifetime? Describe what happened. How has it affected you emotionally? How do you perceive yourself? How has it affected your trust in people?

How has your blaming caused you to lose favor in your work?

How has your blaming driven you from the Lord's presence?

Do you complain a lot? How is your complaining an act of being a victim?

How have you been the perpetrator of victimizing someone else?

Chapter 3

Pride Is a Lie

Randy never knew his real dad; he had abandoned his mother before Randy was born. His mother married another man and had more children, and his stepdad never treated Randy as his own. His mother was hard on him. It was almost as though she took out the abandonment of his dad on Randy.

Randy grew up, married, and had two sons and a good job. But he spent more than he made, so he embezzled from his employer and wrote bad checks, thinking that no one would find out. Randy was sent to prison in his early twenties. He didn't learn his lesson from his first prison sentence and was sent back again for a second. The second time in prison, he claimed to have found the Lord and now professed Christ as his Lord. Unfortunately, his wife divorced him before his release.

Randy was released from prison and moved to another state for a fresh start. He joined a church and found new friends. But for Randy, nothing changed on the inside. He continued to live a life of rejection, even though he professed to be a Christian. He was overly critical of others. He continuously offended others by accusing them of talking behind his back and spreading evil lies about him. He regularly judged the character of others and truthfulness of their lives. He continually professed to see the hidden pitfalls and deceptive agendas of others. He always had a list of people whom he rejected, criticized, and did not trust.

Even though Randy was very intelligent, organized, and capable, he went from job to job. There was always some hidden reason why his employer let him go. Even after being sent to prison twice for embezzlement, he continued to dishonestly manipulate his employers' finances to his own gain. Instead of reporting him and having to prove his guilt, they just fired him. Randy never confessed to any of his hidden evil behaviors. On the outside, he portrayed himself as an upstanding Christian. And he continually pointed out the faults of others and his mistrust in them. But his hidden life was filled with willful sin that he thought no one knew about.

What Is Pride?

We usually think of a prideful person as someone who thinks too highly of himself. Satan began as a magnificent and beautiful angel. His fall was pride, and his pride was a direct consequence of his focus on his own beauty (Ezekiel 28:17). He believed a lie about himself. A victim becomes prideful but with a twisted point of view. The Devil's pride grew out of the perfection given to him by God. He was a "model of perfection" and "full of wisdom and perfect in beauty" (Ezekiel 28:12). His perfection, wisdom, and beauty were part of his created being. You would think that would have been enough for him, but he wanted a higher status; he wanted to be raised up above God (Isaiah 14:12–14). So he proceeded to establish his own kingdom, where he would be at the top in submission to no one and with everyone in submission to him.

We normally don't think of the victim as being at the top. By definition, a victim has been attacked, abused, short-changed, and brought low. How could the victim be prideful? However, in a perverted way, the victim, like Randy, raises himself up by condemning those around him. It is a lie either way. We can lie about ourselves by putting ourselves above others. Or we can lie about others by putting them below ourselves.

In either case, the victim has effectively put himself in a higher place as compared to others. It is an excuse to rule, to be in control. One with a victim mentality typically seeks to be the one in control. He may control through intimidating anger, even rage. He justifies his anger because he believes himself to be the victim, not the aggressor. Therefore, his anger is justified. If he doesn't get everything his way, it is because others are victimizing him. He must retaliate out of self-preservation. Humility is not part of his character. In truth, he has robbed himself of the nature of God.

Randy was guilty of sin and crime, yet he continually accused others of victimizing him. In pride, by blaming others for abusing him, he condoned his own sinful behavior. Jesus spoke against pride numerous times. Jesus was compassionate to sinners, but he rejected the Pharisees because of their pride.

In reading the following parables, it is important to realize that the one who sees himself as a victim has judged those around him. He looks at others with evil intent. He views others as being his evil enemies. To do this he usually has to exaggerate, even lie to himself, about their nature and motives. He is driven to portray others as selfishly taking advantage of him. He is driven to judge them, to lower them, and raise himself. He cannot see the truth about them or himself, because his pride is blinding him. Jesus spoke sharply about such people. Jesus gave two parables on pride. In both, he contrasts the prideful to the humble.

> Do not judge, or you too will be judged. For in the same way you judge others, you will be judged, and with the measure you use, it will be measured to you.
> Why do you look at the speck of sawdust in your brother's eye and pay no attention to the plank in your own eye? How can you say to your brother, "Let me take the speck out of your eye," when all the time there is a plank in your own eye? You hypocrite, first take the plank out of your own eye, and then you will see clearly to remove the speck from your brother's eye. (Matthew 7:1–5 NIV)

One with a victim mentality cannot see his own sin, but he continually points out the sins of others. He exaggerates their sin so that he can compare himself to them, thereby raising his view of himself. Jesus spoke of the pride of the Pharisee who saw himself as nearly perfect when he compared himself to a lowly tax collector.

> To some who were confident of their own righteousness and looked down on everybody else, Jesus told this parable: "Two men went up to the temple to pray, one a Pharisee and the other a tax collector. The Pharisee stood up and prayed about himself: 'God, I thank you that I am not like other men—robbers, evildoers, adulterers—or even like this tax collector. I fast twice a week and give a tenth of all I get.'
> "But the tax collector stood at a distance. He would not even

look up to heaven, but beat his breast and said, 'God, have mercy on me, a sinner.'

"I tell you that this man, rather than the other, went home justified before God. For everyone who exalts himself will be humbled, and he who humbles himself will be exalted."
(Luke 18:9–14 NIV)

Victims Are Blind to Themselves

Most victims do not recognize that they are in bondage to their own perceptions. They are forever talking about how someone has offended them, cheated them, violated them, mistreated them, and so on. Their slanderous accusations never seem to end.

One of the strongest signs of a victim comes from his words about others. If he is constantly tearing others down, he probably sees himself as a victim. He inwardly believes that pushing others down will raise himself. Ironically, his slander and complaining about others only pushes himself lower and lower.

Jesus was God, yet he lowered himself to us and subjected himself to our abuse, but he did not become a victim. We are to be like Jesus in his victorious humility.

> Do nothing out of selfish ambition or vain conceit, but in humility consider others better than yourselves. Each of you should look not only to your own interests, but also to the interests of others.
>
> Your attitude should be the same as that of Christ Jesus: Who, being in very nature God, did not consider equality with God something to be grasped, but made himself nothing, taking the very nature of a servant, being made in human likeness. And being found in appearance as a man, he humbled himself and became obedient to death—even death on a cross!
> (Philippians 2:3–8 NIV)

Pride is a lie. Pride is believing that we are something we are not. Humility is not thinking lowly of ourselves; humility is being truthful about ourselves. It is living in the light with nothing hidden. Pride is walking in darkness so that the truth cannot be seen. The darkness of pride lies to us and to others. The victim remains a victim, because he only pretends to be in the light. In reality, he lives his life in secret, hiding his behavior and secret agendas from others. Inside he is sick, but he doesn't want anyone to know, so he portrays himself as being on top of things. But inwardly, he never stops struggling.

Exposing what is hidden brings about true freedom and healing. But to the prideful, this is too fearful. The prideful do not trust enough to come out into the open in humility.

John wrote about true fellowship with God. He said that it begins with open fellowship with one another. It requires us to come out of hiding in darkness and into the light, where nothing can hide. Jesus is this light, and we come into this light by confessing what is really in our hearts and minds to other Christian brothers and sisters, who are also coming out of darkness into the light.

> This is the message we have heard from him and declare to you: God is light; in him there is no darkness at all. If we claim to have fellowship with him yet walk in the darkness, we lie and do not live by the truth.
>
> But if we walk in the light, as he is in the light, we have fellowship with one another, and the blood of Jesus, his Son, purifies us from all sin. If we claim to be without sin, we deceive ourselves and the truth is not in us. If we confess our sins, he is faithful and just and will forgive us our sins and purify us from all unrighteousness. If we claim we have not sinned, we make him out to be a liar and his word has no place in our lives. (1 John 1:5–10 NIV)

When we are wounded inside, we may also carry a great amount of shame as well. The shame drives us to hide what is inside and to portray a different person on the outside who is more acceptable and honored. But this only causes more shame and crippled behavior. The key to healing is not hiding but exposure to those who love us. James wrote about how to be healed.

> Therefore confess your sins to each other and pray for each other so that you may be healed. The prayer of a righteous man is powerful and effective. (James 5:16 NIV)

The reality is that we are all sinners, struggling with our past and our present behavior. We are in this battle against sin together, and together we gain the victory. The victory comes from openly trusting one another with our true self. It comes from loving each other, not judging and condemning each other. It comes from forgiving one another and carrying the burdens of our brother's soul.

> Therefore, as God's chosen people, holy and dearly loved, clothe yourselves with compassion, kindness, humility, gentleness and patience. Bear with each other and forgive whatever grievances you may have against one another. Forgive as the Lord forgave you. And over all these virtues put on love, which binds them all together in perfect unity. (Colossians 3:12–14 NIV)

Pride separates. Humility unites. Pride hides. Humility draw us close. Pride does not love. Humility carries the burdens of others. Pride compares and rejects. Humility gives us something to be truly proud about, a repentant, nonjudgmental heart. Pride is the sign of a victim. Humility is the sign of victory. In humility, we bring victory to others as well.

> Brothers, if someone is caught in a sin, you who are spiritual should restore him gently. But watch yourself, or you also may be tempted. Carry each other's burdens, and in this way you will fulfill the law of Christ. If anyone thinks he is something when he is nothing, he deceives himself. Each one should test his own actions. Then he can take pride in himself, without comparing himself to somebody else, for each one should carry his own load. (Galatians 6:1–5 NIV)

Pride will bring us down. Humility will bring us victory. The victim is afraid that he will lose control if he gives in to the will of others, so he strives in his own strength to be on top of others. The true victor knows that he will lose his victory if he gives in to his own fears, so he trusts in God. Humility is victorious over pride.

> Pride goes before destruction, and a haughty spirit before a fall. It is better to be of a lowly spirit with the poor than to divide the spoil with the proud. (Proverbs 16:18–19 ESV)

Reflection Questions

Do you find yourself regularly finding fault with others? What does this reveal about you?

What is the evidence of your pride? Of your humility?

How are you willing to suffer for Christ? Where have you?

How is Christ your identity? Compare God's view of you and people's view of you, and how it matters to you.

What have you learned about your victim mentality from your pride or humility?

Chapter 4

Grumbling
and
Complaining

Ed consistently sees the negative in most any situation. It may be a beautiful sunny day. I'll greet him, "Isn't this a beautiful day?" And he will respond, "It's supposed to rain tomorrow." No matter what the conversation, he finds something negative to complain about. He doesn't swear around me, but everything is "friggin' this and friggin' that." His demeanor portrays disgust about people and situations. There is always something in his life to complain about, and the complaint usually reflects on someone else. Thankfulness is essentially nonexistent. In his youth, he was a victim of a dysfunctional broken home, and now he sees himself as a victim. His first marriage did not work, and it is not too difficult to see how it must have been steeped with complaining about everything and each other. He is not a happy man. It really does not matter what his circumstances, he sees himself as under attack—as a loser. He has chosen to believe a host of lies. His grumbling and complaining come from a victim's heart. Grumbling and complaining feed his angry soul. He will never become victorious until he repents of his lack of thankfulness.

The Origin of Grumbling and Complaining

Why do we grumble and complain so much? What is the state of our heart? Grumbling and complaining have the same origin as viewing ourselves as victims.

Grumbling and complaining are common to all of us. Normally we feel justified to complain and gripe. After all, aren't we the ones who have been cheated and abused by others? We are the victim! Why should we be blamed for verbalizing what others have done to us? But if we could see the true motives of our hearts, we would have a different viewpoint. The Bible speaks very strongly about grumbling and complaining. It is much more serious than most of us think.

Grumbling and complaining are forms of anger. It may not be violent or hot-tempered, but it can be driven by the same selfish motivation. We are commanded not to argue or complain so that we can become blameless and pure.

> Do everything without complaining or arguing, so that you may become blameless and pure, children of God without fault in a crooked and depraved generation, in which you shine like stars in the universe … (Philippians 2:14–15 NIV)

Grumbling and complaining are the opposite of thankfulness. It is forever looking at life and proclaiming that all is bad and that we have been cheated and abused by someone. In essence we are saying, "You don't love me!" The grumbling proclaims that he is not loved—by God or others.

Grumbling and complaining are rebellions against God. This picture is clearly seen from a study of the Israelites.

God's people, the Israelites, had grown to a great number in Egypt. The Egyptians had become fearful of their powerful numbers, so they subjected them to harsh slavery. They had been in this bondage for four hundred years, when God sent Moses to deliver them from their suffering. God sent ten miraculous plagues before Pharaoh finally let them go. But as they left, Pharaoh had a change of heart and sent his armies after them. Again God delivered them by parting the Red Sea, so his people could cross over on dry land. But then he allowed the water to come crashing down on the Egyptian army who was in pursuit.

Then God led them across the desert to a lush land that he had promised to give them. When they got there, they sent twelve men to spy out the land. They came back with glowing reports about how it was everything that God had promised. However, it was already inhabited. God promised to deliver the land into their hands, but ten of the twelve spies were afraid and recommended that they not go in. They did not believe God would bring them victory, even though they had just witnessed such a great deliverance from Egyptian bondage. So God sent them back out into the desert for forty years, until this unbelieving rebellious generation died off.

That is a brief summary of the account. Now let's look deeper into the Scriptures to see the nature of their grumbling and complaining.

The Israelites had just seen God's powerful hand with the ten plagues and the parting of the Red Sea. They had traveled just three days into the desert when they began to grumble and complain.

> Then Moses led Israel from the Red Sea and they went into the Desert of Shur. For three days they traveled in the desert without finding water. When they came to Marah, they could not drink its water because it was bitter. (That is why the place is called Marah.) So the people grumbled against Moses, saying, "What are we to drink?"
>
> Then Moses cried out to the LORD, and the LORD showed him a piece of wood. He threw it into the water, and the water became sweet. (Exodus 15:22–25 NIV)

Grumbling and complaining is a grievous sin. The Israelites wandered in the desert for forty years and lost their opportunity to enter the Promised Land because of their rebellious grumbling and complaining. We are warned today not to fall as they did (Hebrews 3:7–4:11). These verses will give a deeper look into what happened: Exodus 15:24–17:3; Numbers 14:1–36, 16:11, 16:41, 17:5, 17:10; Deut. 1:27; Psalm 78, 106:25; James 5:9; Jude 16; Romans 13:1–7; 1 Corinthians 10:10).

The Israelites overflowed with complaints:

No Food: They had only been out of Egypt one and a half months, and they were ready to go back into bondage. (Read Exodus 16:1–16.) Instead of being thankful for their freedom, they complained about not having any food. They did not trust that God loved them and would feed them. They grumbled and complained about Moses and Aaron, but God heard their complaints and took them as against him. This should be a warning for us;

when we grumble and complain to others, about others, or against others, we are really voicing our complaints against God, who supplies all things.

The Israelites grumbled and complained about not having food, and God miraculously provided manna each day. This was an obvious miracle of provision from God. They complained about not having any meat, and God miraculously provided an enormous harvest of quail.

> Now a wind went out from the LORD and drove quail in from the sea. It brought them down all around the camp to about three feet above the ground, as far as a day's walk in any direction. (Numbers 11:31 NIV)

No Water: One would think that by this time they would stop their faithless grumbling and complaining and trust in God to provide whatever they needed. But that was not the case. They were in the desert, and they became thirsty. Instead of seeking the Lord for water, they quarreled and complained to Moses again.

> The whole Israelite community set out from the Desert of Sin, traveling from place to place as the LORD commanded. They camped at Rephidim, but there was no water for the people to drink. So they quarreled with Moses and said, "Give us water to drink."
>
> Moses replied, "Why do you quarrel with me? Why do you put the LORD to the test?"
>
> But the people were thirsty for water there, and they grumbled against Moses. They said, "Why did you bring us up out of Egypt to make us and our children and livestock die of thirst?" (Exodus 17:1–3 NIV)

God was angry about their complaints and lack of faith in his love for them, but he provided water for them anyway. Moses struck a rock, and water gushed out.

Fear of Enemies: The Lord brought his people across the desert to the land of promise. Twelve spies went in to check it out, and they came back with two reports. One, the land is everything that God promised. It was a lush and beautiful land, filled with vegetation. Two, it was also inhabited by large, powerful people. If they wanted the land, they would have to fight for it. Again, one would think that by this time God would have sufficiently proven himself to these people. You would think they would have trusted in his protection, deliverance, and provision. He faithfully demonstrated all three with his deliverance in Egypt and the crossing in the desert. He never let them down. But they continued to grumble and complain. They complained about food, and God fed them. They complained about water, and God provided water in the desert. Now they were complaining about dying at the hands of their enemies.

They even accused God, saying that God brought them this far in order to destroy them by attacks from their enemies. They rejected Moses, the leader God provided, and devised to find a leader of their own choosing.

> That night all the people of the community raised their voices and wept aloud. All the Israelites grumbled against Moses and Aaron, and the whole assembly said to them, "If only we had died in Egypt! Or in this desert! Why is the LORD bringing us to this land only to let us fall by the sword? Our wives and children will be taken as plunder. Wouldn't it be better for us to go back to Egypt?" And they said to each other, "We should choose a leader and go back to Egypt." (Numbers 14:1–4 NIV)

> But you were unwilling to go up; you rebelled against the command of the LORD your God. You grumbled in your tents and said, "The LORD hates us; so he brought us out of Egypt to deliver us into the hands of the Amorites to destroy us. Where can we go? Our brothers have made us lose heart. They say, 'The people are stronger and taller than we are; the cities are large, with walls up to the sky. We even saw the Anakites there.'"
> (Deuteronomy 1:26–28 NIV)

These were a rebellious people, not trusting in God's love for them. They were not thankful for anything that God had done for them. Rather, they grumbled and complained about every aspect of their situation. They saw themselves as victims. They even accused God of hating them—the one who loved them and delivered them. They had completely forgotten how God delivered them from their bondage in Egypt, how God provided food and water in the desert. And now they had forgotten how God promised to them a fruitful land of their own (Exodus 3:17). They did not believe God or trust in his love for them—so they grumbled and complained.

Against Moses and Aaron: God had blessed his people by giving them two anointed leaders. God had demonstrated their anointing in Egypt through the ten plagues and the parting of the Red Sea. But whenever anything happened that the Israelites did not like, they harshly complained to and about their leaders. Moses had told them that the earth would open up and swallow all who opposed their leadership as a witness that they had been chosen by God. Even after this actually came true as the earth swallowed up 250 men before their eyes, they still complained about Moses' and Aaron's leadership (Numbers 16:28–41).

> The next day the whole Israelite community grumbled against Moses and Aaron. "You have killed the LORD'S people," they said. (Numbers 16:41 NIV)

How often do we grumble and complain about the leaders placed over us? We complain about our boss, our president, governor, representatives, judges, parents, spouses, church leaders, and so on.

This is not to say that our leaders are perfect. On the contrary, our leaders are fallen from perfection just as we are. One aspect of that fall is our dishonor of those in authority. The Israelites did not honor Moses, who was chosen by God to rule over them. We must all come to realize that all authority comes from God, it is God who appoints leaders, and it is God who bestows authority upon them. Any complaint against them is a complaint against God.

> Everyone must submit himself to the governing authorities, for there is no authority except that which God has established. The authorities that exist have been established by God. Consequently, he who rebels against the authority is rebelling against what God has instituted, and those who do so will bring judgment on themselves. (Romans 13:1–7 NIV)

Against God: Actually, all grumbling and complaining are ultimately against God. It is God who is our provider and protector. We walk in his steps. He is the one who determines our place in life. He is the one who puts parents, government leaders, bosses, and others over us. It is his authority that controls our lives. When we complain against any of these, we are ultimately complaining to God about the life he has given to us.

The Israelites did not see their complaints as against God but against Moses and Aaron. But that is not how God saw it.

So Moses and Aaron said to all the Israelites, "In the evening you will know that it was the LORD who brought you out of Egypt, and in the morning you will see the glory of the LORD, because he has heard your grumbling against him. Who are we, that you should grumble against us?" Moses also said, "You will know that it was the LORD when he gives you meat to eat in the evening and all the bread you want in the morning, because he has heard your grumbling against him. Who are we? You are not grumbling against us, but against the LORD."

Then Moses told Aaron, "Say to the entire Israelite community, 'Come before the LORD, for he has heard your grumbling.'"

While Aaron was speaking to the whole Israelite community, they looked toward the desert, and there was the glory of the LORD appearing in the cloud.

The LORD said to Moses, "I have heard the grumbling of the Israelites. Tell them, 'At twilight you will eat meat, and in the morning you will be filled with bread. Then you will know that I am the LORD your God.'" (Exodus 16:6–12 NIV)

Thankfulness, the Opposite of Complaining

The Israelites had been victims of Egyptian slavery for four hundred years. They saw themselves as victims. They had numerous generations of victimized slavery, and now they were free. But in their hearts, they were still victims. Life is filled with hardships and blessings. We can focus on the hardships, or we can focus on the blessings. The Israelites only saw the hardships, and their victim mentality blinded them from seeing the blessings, the love, the provision, the protection, and the guidance of God Almighty.

The opposite of grumbling and complaining is thankfulness. The antidote to grumbling and complaining is thankfulness. We should be thankful to and for those around us, but just as complaining about our earthly leaders and providers is a complaint directly to God, thankfulness for anything upon this earth is thankfulness to God, who provides those blessings. It is good to thank those whom God uses to bless us, but it is more important to recognize that God—who is love, who loves us—is the one who is blessing us through others.

Caution: Hypocritical thanksgiving does not fool God. A hypocrite is someone who says one thing but does another. If you grumble and complain about your job all day, and then thank God at the dinner table for providing for your material welfare, are you not a hypocrite? If you complain about your government in your circle of friends, and then thank God for living in this free country, are you not a hypocrite? If you complain and speak evil about your spouse to others, and then tell her you love her, are you not a hypocrite?

A victim is a victim in his heart. Grumbling and complaining are from the heart. True thankfulness is from the heart. We are commanded to always be joyful, to pray at all times, and to be thankful no matter what our circumstances.

> Be joyful always; pray continually; give thanks in all circumstances,
> for this is God's will for you in Christ Jesus.
> (1 Thessalonians 5:16–18 NIV)

God does not bless us one day and curse us the next. He does not hear our prayers one day and ignore us the next. He is always attentive to the prayers of his people, so we can thank him each and every day in every circumstance. He is there with us in our deepest struggles and our most restful pleasures. Contentment is a sign of being truly thankful and truly trusting God with the life he has given us. Contentment is a sign that we have given our lives to God and trust in his loving provision for us.

Paul was falsely accused and sent to prison. From prison he wrote the Philippian church and instructed them to be joyful, thankful, and content in all circumstances. Paul did not see himself as a victim. Neither should we if we want to be set free.

> Rejoice in the Lord always. I will say it again: Rejoice! Let your gentleness be evident to all. The Lord is near. Do not be anxious about anything, but in everything, by prayer and petition, with thanksgiving, present your requests to God. And the peace of God, which transcends all understanding, will guard your hearts and your minds in Christ Jesus. (Philippians 4:4–7 NIV)

> I am not saying this because I am in need, for I have learned to be content whatever the circumstances. I know what it is to be in need, and I know what it is to have plenty. I have learned the secret of being content in any and every situation, whether well fed or

hungry, whether living in plenty or in want. I can do everything through him who gives me strength. (Philippians 4:11–13 NIV)

Paul's identity was in Christ, who died for him, who gave him his Spirit, who purchased the hope of eternal life as we reign with him in God's kingdom. He was joyful and thankful. He was not a grumbler, complainer, or fault finder.

We all need to repent of our grumbling and complaining and to worship God by focusing on all that he has done for us, and all the ways he has blessed us. Thankfulness is the true antidote for our grumbling and complaining. If we grumble and complain to others, we are doing it unto God. In like manner, our thankfulness is an attitude about God's love for us. It is shown when we thank others as well as when we thank God directly. If we walk in thankfulness, our victim disposition will subside.

This is a spiritual battle. As thanks is to God, so complaining is to the devil.

Disciplines:

• Set aside time each day to meditate on your blessings. Confess your blessings to God, and express your appreciation and thankfulness.
• Imagine the effects on others (friends, family, supervisor, fellow workers). Become a blessing to others with your appreciative and joyful attitude about your life and your situations—all of them, easy or difficult.

Reflection Questions

How many times a day do you complain?

How is your complaining a sign of your view of yourself as a victim? Who or what do you complain about the most? How does your complaining about them describe you as their victim?

How many times a day do you thank God for his blessings to you?

Do you blame or complain about others? Your boss? Fellow workers? Family and friends? Government officials? Anyone in authority?

How would it change your view of yourself if you were thankful in all things?

Chapter 5

Exempt from God's Command to Love

James and Karen have been proclaiming Christians for many years. James is a hardworking and faithful Christian husband. They have several fine, God-fearing children. Karen's childhood was filled with anger and emotional abuse, but her married life has had no significant hardships. James is not into drugs or alcohol. He is not physically abusive. He is an excellent provider. His emotions are within normal control. However, Karen expected more of him and from him. Their personalities are opposites. He's an introvert, and she's an extrovert. When conflict occurs, she attacks and he retreats. He sees himself as a victim of her anger and complaints. She sees herself as a victim of his selfishness. She does not feel loved, because he spends too much time by himself, works too many hours, and avoids interactions. They both feel rejected and victimized.

After over twenty years of marriage, Karen had decided not to continue to be a victim. She left him. Jesus clearly spoke against divorce, but she feels totally justified. Her reasoning goes like this:

> I am a victim of my husband's emotional abuse. It is tearing me up inside, and my relationship with the Lord is at stake. I am becoming more and more distant from God due to the anger,

anxiety, depression, resentment, disappointment, and bitterness caused by my husband's abuse. I must escape my husband's grasp on me so that I can obtain inner healing and return to the Lord. God has told me to leave him so that I could return to Him.

James thinks Karen is the whole problem; "I do not need to repent." Karen thinks, *I am being abused!* Karen thinks James is the whole problem: "I do not need to repent. Jesus does not want me to suffer under the abuse of a sinful spouse. He wants me to leave him for my own emotional safety." "Don't judge me," is used by both to deny any wrongdoing or reason to repent.

Victims are "always right" in their accusations and decisions. Victims do not see their own sin; it is always justified due to the abuse caused by someone else's sin. Victims do not believe that Jesus expects us to suffer at the hands of others; therefore, they are justified in rejecting and attacking anyone who brings suffering into their lives. They also feel justified in holding onto bitterness and unforgiveness. Even though they refuse to be judged, they will judge others and justify themselves because they are victims.

My wife and I have counseled many marriages. God is faithful, and he will heal any marriage if both the husband and wife are humble and repentant. The couples that never seem to make progress are the ones in which one or both of them have concluded that they are the victim in the marriage. In other words, one of them, or both of them, see the partner as being 90 percent of the problem. They are essentially pointing at each other, proclaiming their spouse to be the reason for their conflict.

Jesus came so that we would be victorious over sin. Proclaiming to be a victim never brings victory. The world as led by the Devil proclaims the opposite. The world tells us that victory comes from being the strongest and not letting others take advantage of us. You must fight! You must stand your ground! You must proclaim yourself as the righteous one and others as evil perpetrators.

This mode of thinking dissolves any responsibility to love. Jesus commanded us to love one another. He even commanded us to love our enemies. How much more should we love our spouse?

> A new command I give you: Love one another. As I have loved you, so you must love one another. By this all men will know that you are my disciples, if you love one another. (John 13:34–35 NIV)

But I tell you who hear me: Love your enemies, do good to those who hate you, bless those who curse you, pray for those who mistreat you. If someone strikes you on one cheek, turn to him the other also. If someone takes your cloak, do not stop him from taking your tunic. Give to everyone who asks you, and if anyone takes what belongs to you, do not demand it back. Do to others as you would have them do to you.

If you love those who love you, what credit is that to you? Even "sinners" love those who love them. And if you do good to those who are good to you, what credit is that to you? Even "sinners" do that. And if you lend to those from whom you expect repayment, what credit is that to you? Even "sinners" lend to "sinners," expecting to be repaid in full. But love your enemies, do good to them, and lend to them without expecting to get anything back. Then your reward will be great, and you will be sons of the Most High, because he is kind to the ungrateful and wicked. Be merciful, just as your Father is merciful. (Luke 6:27–36 NIV)

The victim says, "I am a victim. I am not the one who needs to love. Others need to love me." It is an excuse—a lie to self—that allows disobedience and selfishness.

We counseled a couple where the wife confessed all sorts of victimizations from her younger years: divorced parents, abandonment, rejection, her own divorce by her first husband, and so on. She was in her second marriage, and she accused her husband of a suspected adulterous affair several years ago (I am not sure it actually occurred), and they were still dealing with it. Actually, she was still holding onto it with a tight grip. She was openly obnoxious, critical, rejecting, controlling, vindictive, and condemning. She was clearly a major problem in their marriage. But she made sure that her husband knew she was the victim in their marriage. All responsibility to repent was his. She used this lever to manipulate the smallest details of his behavior. She was never pleased with him, and he was forever trying not to offend her. Adultery is always a serious sin in any marriage, but her selfish, manipulating pride was just as serious. She had convinced herself that she had no need to love her husband, because she was the victim. Now he had to carry the burden of all the love for both of them. This is not a picture of a unified marriage.

Loving one another is foundational for being a Christian. Without sacrificial love, we are not Christians. Confessions and professions do not make up for our lack of love. Jesus said,

> If you love me, you will obey what I command.
> (John 14:15 NIV)

> As the Father has loved me, so have I loved you. Now remain in my love. If you obey my commands, you will remain in my love, just as I have obeyed my Father's commands and remain in his love. I have told you this so that my joy may be in you and that your joy may be complete. My command is this: Love each other as I have loved you. Greater love has no one than this, that he lay down his life for his friends. You are my friends if you do what I command. (John 15:9–14 NIV)

The victim deceives himself into thinking that he is the victim, so he is the one to be loved. Everyone else is obligated to love him. He puts himself in a place of being in control of his own blessings from others.

In reality, the exact opposite occurs. First, love cannot be demanded; it must be a voluntary action. Manipulating someone else's actions toward us does not bring true love. Neither does it bring about security. Ultimate security is only found in trusting God's love for us. However, we come to know God's love when we submit to his command to love one another.

Look at the words of Jesus again. What do we gain from obeying his command to love one another? We remain in Jesus' love and the Father's love. We will obtain complete joy from Jesus' joy. We become friends of Jesus. All of these promised blessings are lost if we do not obey his command to love one another. *The victim cuts himself off from receiving these blessings, and, ironically, if he did receive them, he would find that he has no need to be a victim. He struggles with being in control of his blessings versus obeying Jesus and trusting God for his blessings.*

John understood love and he wrote extensively on it. He gives further blessings that come from obediently loving one another.

> Dear friends, let us love one another, for love comes from God. Everyone who loves has been born of God and knows God. Whoever does not love does not know God, because God is love. This is how God showed his love among us: He sent his one and only Son into the world that we might live through him. This is

love: not that we loved God, but that he loved us and sent his Son as an atoning sacrifice for our sins. Dear friends, since God so loved us, we also ought to love one another. No one has ever seen God; but if we love one another, God lives in us and his love is made complete in us. (1 John 4:7–12 NIV)

Victims live as though they are exempt from Jesus' command to love. What they do not realize is that their disobedience is sowing for them a separation from God, and they are headed toward death on the inside and for eternity. We already saw how Cain murdered his own brother, Abel, because he was jealous of God's favor for him. Cain saw himself as a victim and, therefore, justified his hatred for his brother and murdered him. In the end, he was even further from God and with less favor, and his life was cursed. All self-proclaiming victims can fall into this same deception. They can readily justify their offenses against others, because they are the proclaiming victim. They may think that they deserve to be on top, but they have sown the seeds for their own destruction with no one to blame but themselves.

This is the message you heard from the beginning: We should love one another. Do not be like Cain, who belonged to the evil one and murdered his brother. And why did he murder him? Because his own actions were evil and his brother's were righteous. Do not be surprised, my brothers, if the world hates you. We know that we have passed from death to life, because we love our brothers. Anyone who does not love remains in death. Anyone who hates his brother is a murderer, and you know that no murderer has eternal life in him. (1 John 3:11–15 NIV)

It should be clear from the previous passage (1 John 4:7–12) that in order to know God, we must love one another. Eternal life is obtained by knowing God through Jesus. God is love. The only way to know him is to love. Jesus said,

Now this is eternal life: that they may know you, the only true God, and Jesus Christ, whom you have sent. (John 17:3 NIV)

Eternal life comes from knowing God. Knowing God comes by obediently loving one another. So the one who does not love has cut himself off from knowing God and receiving his eternal life within. John wrote that if we love one another, God lives in us, and his love is made complete in us. The victim does not experience God living within him, and his love is never made complete.

The victim sees himself as being under the attack of others, but it is the victim himself who has done the most harm to himself by cutting himself off from the powerful grace of God working in his very soul.

Paul wrote to the Ephesians, telling them about how they could know God's vast love and how they could be filled with the whole nature of God.

> I pray that out of his glorious riches he may strengthen you with power through his Spirit in your inner being, so that Christ may dwell in your hearts through faith. And I pray that you, being rooted and established in love, may have power, together with all the saints, to grasp how wide and long and high and deep is the love of Christ, and to know this love that surpasses knowledge— that you may be filled to the measure of all the fullness of God. (Ephesians 3:16–19 NIV)

Paul states that we would be "strengthened with power," that we would be "filled to the measure of all the fullness of God," and that we would "know God's love that surpasses knowledge." All of this comes as a consequence of "being rooted and established in love."

The victim believes that he is in control of his blessings of love by manipulating the love of others for him through his anger, whining, and complaining. In reality, his insecurity comes from *not* knowing God's love that is only fully realized by being rooted and established in his own love for others, not in other's love for him.

God created all of us with two basic needs: one, to be loved. The other is to love others. Both are basic needs for the essence of life. We cannot control the first, the love of others for us. But we can control the latter, our love for others. Jesus commands us to love one another. If we all obediently and sacrificially loved one another, both basic needs would be fulfilled among us. On the contrary, if we all live as though we are the ones who should be loved, we will all come up short. That is the ultimate victimization, when we all fail to love one another and spiritually die.

Reflection Questions

Do you perceive yourself as being shortchanged of love? How do you justify your view?

Are you easily hurt, with the thinking or attitude that you have been offended? In other words, someone should have loved you, but you were not loved. What are some situations where you were hurt by others? How did you perceive yourself a victim?

How do you treat those who hurt your feelings (anger, rejection, criticism, or forgiveness, love, and acceptance)?

How does your perception as a victim cheat you out of blessings?

What would you have to do to give up being a proclaiming victim?

Chapter 6

Exempt from Forgiving

I knew Greg from prison. I first met him when he came to one of our Bible based classes on anger (Freedom from Anger). Greg was a big, white man in his late twenties. When he first arrived, he was sullen and distraught. He never smiled. When each student introduced himself, Greg proclaimed that he was not a Christian, but that he needed something, so he decided to see what our class had to offer him.

In the course of each man sharing the background of their anger problems and who they might have to forgive, Greg spoke up quite strongly. He stated that he hated his father for what he saw him do to his mother and for how his dad treated him. Greg said that it was like his father took his heart out and stomped it on the floor. He said he hated him and could never forgive him.

I told Greg in front of the group that I was praying for him, and all of his fellow inmates—about a dozen others—said that they were praying for him, too. I put my hand on him and said, "Greg, you don't have a chance." God was going to touch him.

Greg left class but sought the Lord. His father and mother were divorced. His father was also in prison, serving a life sentence for murder. His mother lived in another state. He had not heard from either of them in a few years. He prayed, saying to God, "If you are real, I want to hear from my father and mother." Within a week or two, he received a letter from both of them. From this point, his faith began to grow.

We always began class by asking one of the prisoners to open in prayer. To our surprise, Greg immediately volunteered. He began by thanking God for speaking to him the past week. When he was finished, I asked him if he could share how God spoke to him. He shared that God came to him while he lay alone on his bunk. I wish I had written down his exact words, but it was to the effect that God had been pleased that he came to him and how God had been longing for this day to come into his life.

A week or so later, Greg told us that he wrote his dad, asking him to forgive him for being such a terrible son. This is the son who just a few weeks earlier said that he hated his dad for being such a terrible father.

Then he came to class and told us that his father wrote him back, asking for Greg to forgive him for being such a terrible father. Greg said that he knew his father was crying when he wrote it, because the ink was running down the page. We all were holding back our tears at his statement.

Greg's entire demeanor had changed. He no longer came to class sullen but with joy. Within a few weeks, he was water baptized into Christ. He told us that his goal was to be released from prison and to visit his dad and restore a relationship with him.

Greg was set free. He was a victim as a child, but the most serious victimization was not what happened on the outside but the bondage that occurred on his inside. Jesus set him free. Unforgiveness was his captivity. Forgiveness set him free. He became victorious in Jesus Christ.

Greg was clearly a victim of his father's anger as a defenseless child. If we knew the exact details of his experiences, we might even be inclined to agree that Greg was justified to hold his father in judgment and to hold onto the offenses. It is very easy for any of us to be so helplessly offended as to justify our hatred and grudges. It only seems just. What most of us do not realize is that the greatest victimization was not to our bodies or the past circumstance. The greatest victimization is what is happening at present in our own hearts and minds. Most child abuse does not leave the child physically handicapped for his lifetime. The child heals from the physical abuse quite readily. But the wounds to the heart can linger for a lifetime. Healing only occurs with forgiveness. Time does not heal. Drugs and alcohol only cover up. Outbursts of anger do not release us from anger; they only feed upon the root cause and make it worse. Practically every relationship that we have will be adversely affected by unforgiveness that lingers from our past. It can destroy a marriage, our children, our friendships, our work, and our relationship with God. *Unforgiveness will cripple our entire life for our entire lifetime.*

In spite of how unforgiveness will destroy our lives, many who have held onto their identity as a victim are unwilling to let go by forgiving. They feel justified, and now their victim identity grants them special privileges in other relationships. They may lack to see their own depravity and their own responsibilities in relationships. Since they are victims, all responsibilities fall on the shoulders of others. They are rewarded for holding onto their unforgiveness. In their view, they have a free excuse to be offensive, unpleasant, accusing, demanding, complaining, and so on. It is like having an adult temper tantrum.

Commanded to Forgive

We must all realize that forgiveness is not optional. Being the offended party does not grant us special privileges in our relationships with others. Victims do not have a special status with God that absolves them of the responsibility to love others, to overlook an offense (Proverbs10:12; 19:11; 1 Peter 4:8) and to forgive. We should be alarmed when we see ourselves as a victim. We should fear for our soul if we are holding someone in unforgiveness. If we do not forgive others when they sin against us, neither will God forgive us. God forgives our sins against him as we forgive those who sin against us.

> Forgive us our debts, as we also have forgiven our debtors. And lead us not into temptation, but deliver us from the evil one.'
>
> For if you forgive men when they sin against you, your heavenly Father will also forgive you. But if you do not forgive men their sins, your Father will not forgive your sins.
> (Matthew 6:12–15 NIV)

Forgiving is not easy. To forgive is a decision to suffer at the hands of the sinner. It is a decision to not play the victim's role. Victims hold onto the offense. *The offense is their identity.* To forgive is to release those who offend us. It is a decision to love those who attack us.

Being a Christian is the most difficult thing we will do. It is not a matter of going to church on Sunday, singing some songs, hearing a sermon, and going home. Christians live for Christ as Christ lived. Jesus instructed us to take up our cross as he took up his cross. Jesus died at the hands of sinners. They ridiculed him, lied about him, slandered him, mocked him, beat and tortured him, and finally, nailed him to a cross to die. Jesus told us to take up our cross when others sin against us.

> And he said to all, "If anyone would come after me, let him deny himself and take up his cross daily and follow me. For whoever would save his life will lose it, but whoever loses his life for my sake will save it. For what does it profit a man if he gains the whole world and loses or forfeits himself? (Luke 9:23–25 ESV)

Jesus went even further in his commands to us. Forgiving our enemies is very difficult, but Jesus commanded us to even love our enemies. He commands us not even to resist their ill-treatment of us.

> You have heard that it was said, "An eye for an eye and a tooth for a tooth." But I say to you, Do not resist the one who is evil. But if anyone slaps you on the right cheek, turn to him the other also. And if anyone would sue you and take your tunic, let him have your cloak as well. And if anyone forces you to go one mile, go with him two miles. Give to the one who begs from you, and do not refuse the one who would borrow from you.
>
> You have heard that it was said, "You shall love your neighbor and hate your enemy." But I say to you, Love your enemies and pray for those who persecute you, so that you may be sons of your Father who is in heaven. For he makes his sun rise on the evil and on the good, and sends rain on the just and on the unjust. For if you love those who love you, what reward do you have? Do not even the tax collectors do the same? And if you greet only your brothers, what more are you doing than others? Do not even the Gentiles do the same? You therefore must be perfect, as your heavenly Father is perfect. (Matthew 5:38–48 ESV)

Jesus is not saying that we should be looking for ways to be abused, as though abuse makes us something special or holy or like God. Jesus' emphasis is not on being abused; his emphasis is on overcoming evil with good. Love is our weapon against those who would mistreat us. Biblical love is always sacrificial. Jesus sacrificed his life so that we could have his life. Jesus commanded us to love as he loved us, and then he said that the greatest love is to lay down our lives for others (John 15:12–13).

It is not always loving to allow someone to abuse us. You are not being loving to the rapist to allow him to rape you. You are not being loving to the thief to leave your car unlocked. We are not to tempt others into sin. On the other hand, what should our response be after we have been abused, mistreated, victimized—sinned against? And what if our perpetrator abuses us over and over, what then? Peter had the same concern.

> Then Peter came up and said to him, "Lord, how often will my brother sin against me, and I forgive him? As many as seven times?" Jesus said to him, "I do not say to you seven times, but seventy times seven.
>
> "Therefore the kingdom of heaven may be compared to a king who wished to settle accounts with his servants. When he began to settle, one was brought to him who owed him ten thousand talents. And since he could not pay, his master ordered him to be sold, with his wife and children and all that he had, and payment to be made. So the servant fell on his knees, imploring him, 'Have patience with me, and I will pay you everything.' And out of pity for him, the master of that servant released him and forgave him the debt. But when that same servant went out, he found one of his fellow servants who owed him a hundred denarii, and seizing him, he began to choke him, saying, 'Pay what you owe.' So his fellow servant fell down and pleaded with him, 'Have patience with me, and I will pay you.' He refused and went and put him in prison until he should pay the debt. When his fellow servants saw what had taken place, they were greatly distressed, and they went and reported to their master all that had taken place. Then his master summoned him and said to him, 'You wicked servant! I forgave you all that debt because you pleaded with me. And should not you have had mercy on your fellow servant, as I had mercy on you?' And in anger his master delivered him to the jailers, until he should pay all his debt. So also my heavenly Father will do to every one of you, if you do not forgive your brother from your heart." (Matthew 18:21–35 ESV)

It really comes down to whether we want to be a disobedient victim or whether we want to be a victorious Christian. We are not victorious when we hold onto an offense. Actually, we are holding onto our status as a victim, and there is no victory in that. The stakes are much higher than the label that we invoke upon ourselves. God has forgiven us. He has chosen not to hold onto our sins at a great cost to himself. He expects us—he commands us—to do the same for those who sin against us. And if we do not obey him and forgive, he will not forgive us. That is the greatest price for holding onto our unforgiving victim status. The abuse is nothing compared to being eternally separated from God, and that is the decision we have made when we hold onto our unforgiving victim status.

True freedom only comes when we can love in the face of evil. Think about Greg again. He came to class in torment and bondage, but when he could forgive and love, he was set free. His torment was replaced with joy. His soul was at stake, but in the end, he became one with Jesus.

Trap of the Devil

The Devil was defeated by the crucifixion of Jesus.

> And having disarmed the powers and authorities, he made a public spectacle of them, triumphing over them by the cross.
> (Colossians 2:15 NIV)

The Devil incited Judas to betray Jesus (John 13:2). So why did he tempt Judas to betray him if he was going to be defeated by the cross?

It is possible that the Devil did not know the power of Jesus' forgiveness for sin by his death on the cross. It is also possible that he assumed that Jesus, being God, would use his powers to protect himself. Jesus could have called on his angels to protect him. Jesus made a conscious and willful choice to die on the cross at the hands of men. He did not even have to allow himself to be apprehended. Let's look at the account.

> Jesus said to him, "Friend, do what you came to do." Then they came up and laid hands on Jesus and seized him. And behold, one of those who were with Jesus stretched out his hand and drew his sword and struck the servant of the high priest and cut off his ear. Then Jesus said to him, "Put your sword back into its place. For all who take the sword will perish by the sword. Do you think that I cannot appeal to my Father, and he will at once send me more than twelve legions of angels? (Matthew 26:50–53 ESV)

Jesus was not a victim of men. He chose to allow men to take his life. In choosing this, he was victorious over the Devil. If he had retaliated, the Devil would have gained the victory. Offense followed by bitter unforgiveness and possibly retaliation is the Devil's power. When we forgive, we disarm the Devil. Jesus did not fail to have victory; he gave up his life willingly in obedience to his heavenly Father.

> The reason my Father loves me is that I lay down my life—only to take it up again. No one takes it from me, but I lay it down of my own accord. I have authority to lay it down and authority to take it up again. This command I received from my Father.
> (John 10:17–18 NIV)

On the cross, as he was looking down on those who hated him, Jesus said, "Father, forgive them, for they do not know what they are doing" (Luke 23:34 NIV). Forgiveness is powerful over evil and the Devil. The Devil's defeat is wrapped up in willful forgiveness.

The Devil does not want us to forgive others. His scheme is to incite an offense that is followed by unforgiveness. If he can succeed in this sequence, he keeps us in captivity. We already inherited a sinful nature from Adam. Offenses are everywhere. We are all sinned upon. What is our victory in this life, since we all sin. First, we have been given his word and his Spirit so we do not continue to sin. But this is a journey; everyone still sins. So how do we have victory in the meantime? The answer is in the power of forgiveness. To forgive is to have victory over the Devil. Paul knew the Devil's schemes, and he knew the power of forgiveness over those schemes.

> If you forgive anyone, I also forgive him. And what I have forgiven—if there was anything to forgive—I have forgiven in the sight of Christ for your sake, in order that Satan might not outwit us. For we are not unaware of his schemes.
> (2 Corinthians 2:10–11 NIV)

Victorious Christians forgive. Victims do not forgive, and become victims of the Devil. That is why Jesus commands us to forgive in order to be forgiven. To hold onto the offense is to serve the Devil, not Jesus. *Forgiveness is always a requirement for deliverance from a victim mentality. Harboring unforgiveness is a setup for becoming a victim.*

Freedom in Jesus

As already discussed, Jesus commanded us to forgive in order to be forgiven. The command to forgive is not legalism. Yes, forgiveness is a decisive action in obedience, but it is not a legalistic work. Rather, it is a work of the Spirit. Harboring an offense is captivity to bitterness, division, and a view of one's self as unloved. Unforgiveness will affect, even cripple, your entire life. Inside we may think that our offender does not deserve to be forgiven, but our unforgiving heart is the heart that suffers most. The unforgiven perpetrator may not even think about his offense. In the meantime, it may be eating at your very soul. *Unforgiveness is captivity. Forgiveness is freedom.*

Jesus came to set the captives free (Luke 4:18–19). Forgiving our offenders is critical for being set free.

Jesus is truth (John 14:6). God's Word is truth. Truth is about God, his creation, and all of life. Jesus came so that we would have this truth about all that exists. Truth is hidden by darkness, lies, and deceptions. Sometimes the greatest darkness is within our own heart. We may experience all our emotions and thoughts, but we may not see what drives them. This kind of darkness can hold us captive to sin, addictions, low self-esteem, anger, hatred, bitterness, depression, hopelessness—and self-victimization.

One who holds onto his identity as a victim is not free; he is captive to a lie. Jesus came to set us free. Forgiveness brings freedom. The truth is that we are all captive and need to be set free by Jesus Christ. We need his light to shine within us so that the darkness is consumed by light. When we can see the truth about our motives and what holds us captive, we can choose to forgive and become released from the bondage of victimization. Jesus is truth, and he is true freedom.

> To the Jews who had believed him, Jesus said, "If you hold to my teaching, you are really my disciples. Then you will know the truth, and the truth will set you free."
>
> They answered him, "We are Abraham's descendants and have never been slaves of anyone. How can you say that we shall be set free?"
>
> Jesus replied, "I tell you the truth, everyone who sins is a slave to sin. Now a slave has no permanent place in the family, but a son belongs to it forever. So if the Son sets you free, you will be free indeed. (John 8:31–36 NIV)

Jesus came so that we could see that our worst perpetrator may be our own heart. Jesus came so that we would have a new heart by the infilling of his Spirit. He came so that we would have a new identity in God as his children. He came so that we would be forgiven and forgive others. He came to bring about the power of the reconciliation of our relationship with God and with one another. He came so that we would have the hope of reigning with Jesus in his kingdom for eternity. He came so that we would have his abundant eternal life.

What is the truth? We are not victims. We are victorious in Jesus Christ.

> No, in all these things we are more than conquerors through him who loved us. (Romans 8:37 NIV)

Reflection Questions

Who are you holding in unforgiveness?

How has your unforgiveness held your own heart captive?

How has the Devil schemed to bring unforgiveness into your heart? How were you set up by him?

Have you thought that your unforgiveness was justified in the eyes of God because you were victimized? What do you think now? What are you going to do about it?

Chapter 7

Justified to Sin

Abuse of all kinds has certainly been on the increase. Sexual abuse within the family is alarming. Many safeguards have been put into place to identify, report, and protect family members from the threat of continued abuse. Sexual abuse has become pandemic. Our prisons are populated with criminal sexual offenders. Men and women who have been sexually abused as children are typically affected the rest of their lives. They view themselves as having been abused, and they continue to label themselves as abused. There is distrust, low self-worth, unforgiveness, and fear, which are understandable.

There can be another dimension to the abuse that is not so obvious, especially with children. It is not the cause of the sexual perpetrator. When someone is going through any kind of hardship, we tend to treat the person as a victim. Compassion is good, but we tend to go beyond compassion. The suffering victim is usually feeling emotional pain, so those around the victim will try to compensate, even to the point of overlooking any undesirable behavior (sin). It is possible to go even further by verbalizing how terrible the abuser must be. As a consequence, not only was the child's body violated, the child's moral character becomes violated.

Hans was the father of two teenage sons and an eleven-year-old daughter, Gretchen. Hans moved from Germany to the United States when Gretchen was just a baby. In Germany, it is common for family members to be naked before each other. They may shower, sauna, beach, and swim in the nude. Certainly this is not commonly accepted in the United States, and Hans was careful about his behavior outside of the home. However, in the home, he did not feel out of place to walk into the bathroom unannounced while his daughter was in the shower. As might be expected, Gretchen talked about her family behavior around school, and a teacher became aware and reported what she heard to the authorities.

Gretchen was a young girl when her father was removed from the home for accusations of sexual abuse. Dad was removed in the middle of the night by two police officers and a social worker. The accusations against her father did not involve any physical sexual contact, but the authorities feared the potential of abuse. A court order kept her dad from coming back home.

Prior to this incident, Gretchen appeared joyful, happy, and sincerely close to her dad. Following this incident, Gretchen was inundated with social workers who wanted to uncover anything else that might have happened. Counselors were provided to help her understand how terribly abused she was and how her father was an unloving sexual pervert who did not love her. The court system defined her dad as a criminal who violated his own daughter. This cycle of reinforcing a view of an abuse victim by social workers, counselors, and court officials went on for over two years. The court officials never did allow Dad to come home.

In time, Gretchen came to hate her dad. She never saw herself as a victim prior to this episode, but afterward, everyone in authority, even a female judge, confirmed her status. Gretchen took upon herself the identity of a victim. As her victim identity grew, so did her hatred for her dad.

All of the professionals, the counselors, social workers, attorneys, and the judge were unaware that there was another enemy in the camp, and they were the enemy. They thought that they were protecting her, but they were also destroying any healthy identity she had. In their eyes, she was a victim *with all of the privileges of a victim*. Victims gain a special status. Everyone feels sorry for them because they are a victim.

Gretchen was just an adolescent. A child should never be in control of those around her. She should never have the upper hand over her parents, and she should never receive special treatment over her two brothers. But that is what happened. Now that she was classified as a victim with special status, she could throw a raging temper tantrum and get her way. She frequently accused and fought with her siblings, and Gretchen was always the one to get her way—she was a victim. Her brothers were in constant conflict with her because of the special status given to her by the authorities.

Gretchen was given an unhealthy status as a victim, and as a consequence, every other family member became a victim of the courts. The focus of the court was *not* to restore the family but to protect Gretchen from any potential abuse, although there had been no accusations of criminal sexual conduct, only suspected potential conduct. Everything was done to "protect" Gretchen of what those in authority thought might potentially happen someday. Gretchen's dad was labeled a sexual pervert by those in authority. Gretchen once looked up to her dad; now she looked down in hatred and disgust.

The family became the ultimate victim. The marriage ended in divorce. The children became divided, hurt, and angry with their situation, each other, and particularly with the legal system. All but Gretchen saw this as a legalistic trap of which they could not escape. Her brothers missed their dad and the family structure they once enjoyed.

Gretchen was a well-behaved, joyful, and well-adjusted young girl before all this happened. Now she has learned that victims have special status. They can rebel, misbehave, do poorly in school, become angry, demand special privileges, accuse without retribution, and often receive special attention. She has also learned that if she cannot manipulate her family within her home, she can go to the authorities for leverage. Those in authority have labeled her a victim with special privileges to justify her sin against those around her. This is as much a serious form of abusive victimization as the purported potential sexual abuse that may have occurred if Dad came home.

Sexual abuse is very serious and should always be firmly addressed and dealt with. In many cases, the father should be removed from the home while the family can be restored to a healthy state. What is commonly missed is the damage done to the abused when they are classified as a victim.

A child should never be encouraged to hate her father or mother, no matter what they may have done to them. Also, victims should never be encouraged to view themselves as a victim. Whenever we do encourage a victim mentality, we have also encouraged them to overlook their own sinful behavior. We are all sinners who have sinned against others. And we have all been sinned against by others. To varying degrees, we are all in this struggle of living in a sinful world. The answer is not to elevate some and condemn others. Jesus came to deal with our sin head-on, not with condemnation, but with forgiveness and restoration. Because of sin, we all struggle with mistrust to some degree. Establishing a victim mentality only increases our level of distrust. Distrust gives birth to isolation. We were not created to be isolated but with a basic need to be united. Isolation may become the ultimate victimization.

In no way do we want to minimize a serious abuse by another, whether it is sexual abuse or anything else. But we must be wise to seek restoration, not an identity as a victim of someone else.

Gretchen's dad did abuse his daughter. He violated her visual privacy, regardless of what was acceptable in Germany. Gretchen grew up in the United States, with a different set of cultural norms. Hans should have recognized that his behavior was inappropriate here and respected the privacy of his young daughter. Counselors agreed after many sessions with Hans that he was not a sexual threat. He acted out of ignorance. His boundaries were not well established. And his intent was not to have a sexual experience with his daughter.

It was good that his behavior was brought out into the open, but instead of resolving a serious family situation, it was made worse. The family was destroyed, and Gretchen has a new status as a victim with special privileges. And she now hates her father. Now she has to deal with the bitterness of her soul that was not a previous issue.

Someone may become a victim of an unfortunate circumstance; it doesn't have to be a personal assault. Maybe you have been crippled as the result of a car accident. Maybe you were born with a debilitating disease. Certainly, we need to be compassionate and caring. But we do not raise people up by coddling their hurts or handicaps. Giving people special relational privileges only cripples them more. Overlooking their behavioral shortcomings is not an act of love. *All victims need to become victorious. Coddling only promotes poor character and continued bondage.*

As marriage counselors, my wife and I have counseled many couples who are on their second, third, fourth, and fifth marriages. We ask what they thought went wrong in their previous marriages. I do not recall anyone ever confessing any responsibility for their previous marriage breakups. People on their fourth or fifth marriage typically cannot see that there is a pattern. They do not see that they are a significant cause to the problems in the marital relationship. It always seems to be the other spouse's fault. They were the victim, so they do not see how they have contributed to the downfall of the marriages.

We met with a couple who were both on their second marriage. I'll call them Dick and Jane. Jane had been abused as a child. As she talked about her past, she described herself as abused by her father, abused by her mother, abused by her parents' divorce, abused by her sister (who got special treatment and privileges), abused by her church (which she left), abused by her first husband, and now abused by her second husband. Jane clearly saw herself as a victim in every close relationship from childhood until the present. She did not see any personal responsibility in any of her relationships. All blame was on the other persons.

Jane claimed to have caught her husband in an affair three or four years before, and she had not gotten over it yet (We were not sure that the affair got beyond conversations with each other, mostly in e-mail.) Right from the start, it was clear that she saw the issue as being her husband's behavior.

We have counseled many couples with very serious marriage struggles. We have seen the Lord restore many marriages, no matter how severe the circumstances. The marriages that fail to be restored are not the ones with the most severity. Rather, they are the ones where one or both spouses do not see themselves as a significant part of the relational problem. They do not see their own sin, or they condone their sinful behavior by blaming the spouse. If either spouse continues to see the relational breakdown as primarily the spouse's fault, unity is never restored. In other words, a victim mentality does not bring unity; it divides. The one with the victim mentality may actually be the perpetrator in disguise. "If I am the victim, I can't possibly be responsible."

Jane came to us at her husband's request. For several years, she had been disciplining his misbehavior. When he behaved in any manner that she deemed unacceptable, she punished him by making him leave home for the night. She constantly judged and badgered him for the slightest infraction. If he wasn't perfect, she granted herself permission to become angry, curse, hit him, and command him to go out for a walk until she felt better. The smallest offense could trigger and justify Jane's behavior. If Dick forgot to put the trash out, or if he ate something that was not in her menu plan, she was in a tizzy, and Dick was the bad guy.

Jane saw herself as the victim. She had seen herself as the victim for most of her life, and now, near fifty, she was still manipulating those around her by taking advantage of her victim status. When we addressed her for her responsibility in the breakdown of their marriage, she became angry with us. Now we were the abusers, because we were not compassionate for the pain she has undergone over the years due to her husband's supposed affair.

I am sure that Jane was abused as a child. But I am also sure that Jane has victimized herself by excusing her own sinful behavior because she has believed a lie. The lie says, "I am a victim. I am justified to be an abuser now."

I knew a man whose violent anger destroyed every relationship that he had. His excuse: he was adopted by parents who never loved each other. Granted, it is a terrible thing to be raised by parents who do not love each other. But this man was in his late thirties. He felt that he was justified to be unloving, because he was a victim of unloving parents.

I addressed him one day about his anger. I told him that if he was not delivered from his anger, it would destroy his life. He just pounded his fist and said, "It works for me." He confessed that he did not date anyone anymore, because none of his relationships worked out. He was also fired from his job multiple times because he did not get along with his fellow workers. But in spite of the evidence, he did not see any need get help for changing his behavior. He thrived on his excuse to be violent; he was a "victim."

It may seem backward, but in these cases, it is the victim who needs to repent. We have no excuse to sin, even if we have been a victim of someone's sin against us. When we sin out of our own hurt and then justify our behavior because we have been abused, we are calling good evil and evil good.

> Woe to those who call evil good and good evil, who put darkness for light and light for darkness, who put bitter for sweet and sweet for bitter. (Isaiah 5:20 NIV)

Anyone who makes excuses for his own sin because of the sin of others has proclaimed his sin as good. What did Jesus say our behavior and attitude should be toward those who abuse us?

> But I tell you who hear me: Love your enemies, do good to those who hate you, bless those who curse you, pray for those who mistreat you. If someone strikes you on one cheek, turn to him the other also. If someone takes your cloak, do not stop him from taking your tunic. Give to everyone who asks you, and if anyone takes what belongs to you, do not demand it back. Do to others as you would have them do to you.
>
> If you love those who love you, what credit is that to you? Even

"sinners" love those who love them. And if you do good to those who are good to you, what credit is that to you? Even "sinners" do that. And if you lend to those from whom you expect repayment, what credit is that to you? Even "sinners" lend to "sinners," expecting to be repaid in full. But love your enemies, do good to them, and lend to them without expecting to get anything back. Then your reward will be great, and you will be sons of the Most High, because he is kind to the ungrateful and wicked. Be merciful, just as your Father is merciful. (Luke 6:27–36 NIV)

Is this command difficult? Of course! Why would Jesus command us to love those who abuse us? Because love is always victorious. Victims are never victorious. And where is the victory? First, the victory within your own heart, mind, and soul. Victims are captive to bitterness, self-preservation, low self-esteem, their own sin, selfish relationships, loss of joy and happiness, and a destructive life. Second, loving our enemies brings glory to God. It has the potential to restore others and to heal relationships. It is a pursuit of the kingdom of God. It is a triumphant act of mercy (James 2:13).

Instead of calling your own evil behavior as good, "overcome evil with good." This is the walk of Christ, and anyone who claims to be in him must walk as Jesus did (1 John 2:6).

Do not repay anyone evil for evil. Be careful to do what is right in the eyes of everybody. If it is possible, as far as it depends on you, live at peace with everyone. Do not take revenge, my friends, but leave room for God's wrath, for it is written: "It is mine to avenge; I will repay," says the Lord. On the contrary: "If your enemy is hungry, feed him; if he is thirsty, give him something to drink. In doing this, you will heap burning coals on his head." Do not be overcome by evil, but overcome evil with good.
(Romans 12:17–21 NIV)

Reflection Questions

Do you see yourself as a victim? Do you use this status to justify your sinful behavior?

How does this statement fit you: "My sin is not so bad because of all that has happened to me. I am weak, abused, and rejected; I am justified to have an addiction. I am justified to retaliate, complain, blame, and sulk"?

How has your victim status driven you to sin?

Are you ready to repent? Are you ready to become victorious?

How might your victorious behavior be a blessing to others, to yourself, and to God?

Chapter 8

Emotions Are Lord

Jesus Did Not Submit to His Emotional Pain

Many of us have experienced emotional pain. In many ways, emotional pain is much more difficult to endure than physical pain. Physical pain is localized, and it only affects the body. Emotional pain reaches down to the heart and soul and then it can affect the entire body.

Jesus demonstrated his submission to his heavenly Father. He not only came to earth as a man with the limitations of man, but he also subjected himself to man's sin. Jesus was a willful victim of our sins against him. His greatest suffering began the night before the cross. The emotional pain was so intense that he sweat drops of blood and was near death due to the enormous internal anguish. But Jesus did not consider escape from the pain to be a higher priority than his Father's will for him.

"Father, if you are willing, take this cup from me; yet not my will, but yours be done." An angel from heaven appeared to him and strengthened him. And being in anguish, he prayed more earnestly, and his sweat was like drops of blood falling to the ground. (Luke 22:42–44 NIV)

Jesus willingly came to earth to do his Father's will—regardless of the personal physical and emotional price that he had to endure.

> For I have come down from heaven not to do my will but to do the will of him who sent me. (John 6:38 NIV)

Jesus submitted to his heavenly Father as Lord of his life. In other words, he sacrificed his body, his emotions, his will, and his life for the will of his Father. He demonstrates what it means for us to submit to him as our Lord.

What Is Lordship?

It is easy to say that Jesus is Lord, but what does that really mean? A lord is someone who rules over the people under him. We do not have lords in the United States, so we have not experienced lordship. When we read in the Bible that Jesus is Lord, it is referring to his complete dominance of the entire creation. If he commands the dead to rise, they rise. If he commands evil spirits to flee, they flee. If he commands the wind to cease, it ceases. All of creation is subject to his supreme authority. He is Lord of all.

> The mountains melt like wax before the LORD, before the Lord of all the earth. (Psalm 97:5 NIV)

In all of the earthly creation, only man rebels against Jesus' authority as Lord. So to say that Jesus is Lord is to confess that Jesus is lord of all, which includes me. Victims may verbally proclaim Jesus as Lord, but for all of us, our words must be proven by our actions. If Jesus is really Lord, we will submit to his will. Think of the Lord's Prayer when we recite, "Thy will be done on earth as it is in heaven." Do we really mean what we pray? If Jesus is Lord, we obediently submit our will to his will.

When someone is lord over us, our actions will submit to the lord's demands. If our emotions are lord, our actions will submit to the will of our emotions. If Jesus is Lord, we will not submit to our emotions, but our actions will submit to the lordship of Jesus Christ.

When Emotions Are Lord

Those whose identity is that of a victim see themselves as a lord. They use their supposed victimization as an excuse to disobey, but it goes further than that. They serve another lord—themselves. Their own emotions become lord of their lives. Everything is about how they feel. If they are upset, it is because they are being victimized. They focus on their hurt feelings and justify any offensive or destructive behavior that proceeds from their feelings. It may even be self-destructive behavior, such as gambling, drugs, alcohol, and pornography. Feelings rule. If someone hurts you, you are justified to become angry and retaliate. Retaliation may be with words, violence, unfaithfulness, selfishness, and so on. Emotions become the lord of their life, not Jesus. Jesus commands us to love one another, to love our enemies, to forgive, to be compassionate, to die to self, to pray for our persecutors, to overlook an offense—to sacrifice our self-will. *When emotions are lord, self-gratification rules.*

I knew a very emotional family, the Joneses. The father, the mother and two sons were all consumed by how they were feeling. I had known the Joneses for about thirty years, from the time their children were young until they were adults. Initially, I thought that these were just very tenderhearted people, who had the capacity to feel and identify with other people's pain. And to some degree, this was true. At first, this sensitivity seemed like a good character trait. And certainly being sensitive can be a strength, and being insensitive is cold and uncaring. But this was not strength; it was uncontrolled weakness.

The father died when the kids, David and Dean, were teenagers. When David first heard about his father's sudden death, he burst into a rage of anger and threw a friend across the room, which he later bragged about. He saw his anger as justified and even to be honored. This was just his emotional reaction to his dad's death. He perceived his rage of anger as an acceptable demonstration of his love for his father.

Dean grew up to be a good athlete and student, but his emotions were lord of his life as well. He had a few setbacks. An injury put the stop on his athletic prowess. Since emotions were lord, he assumed that he had to medicate them. He thought that if something is wrong with your body, medicating the problem is simply the right thing to do. If we care about ourselves, we will medicate the problem. This may be true if we are talking about an infection, but if we have this view for medicating our emotions, we can get into serious trouble. And that is just what happened.

Dean medicated his ill emotions with illicit drugs, prescription drugs, and alcohol. He became an addict. He stole things from the people closest to him to finance the purchase of his medication.

Dean submitted himself to several rehab clinics. Each time he proclaimed that he had been delivered. But sobriety was short lived. Several times he proclaimed that God had delivered him, and for a while, he appeared to be victorious. But victory did not last.

I noticed during his times of sobriety that his conversation was still all about himself and how he felt and how things affected him. During sobriety it was all about how good he felt—good emotions. But as time progressed, something would happen to instill bad feelings. He was still the same overly sensitive kid, where emotions were lord of his life. He was still doing all that he could to make himself feel good. He was forever trying to impress others with who he was, even to the point of making up extravagant stories, all for the purpose of manipulating others to have tender emotions toward him. You see, when emotions are lord, you want others to feel for you. When the emotional slave is feeling good, he wants everyone to feel good alongside him. If he is feeling bad, he wants others to feel bad with him by sharing the pain. He uses his emotions to gain sympathy and control. He is lord.

On the surface, sympathy may seem like a Christian thing to do. Being compassionate and sympathetic can be an act of caring love. But what if you are being manipulated? What if Dean was telling made-up stories just so we would feel sorry for him? And that is just what Dean had done. Some lies were to make us rejoice for him. Some were to make us feel sorry, even grieve with him. But in time, we found that the stories were fictitious, just to get us on his emotional side.

Dean was playing the role of an emotional victim. He had assumed that he was the unfortunate one who needed to feel good at any expense. When God made him feel good, he was praising God. When life got hard and disappointing, he reverted to manipulative lies and drugs. Emotions were always lord of his life. His own wife and children have had to pay the price for his behavior.

We all struggle with our emotions. Certainly we all would prefer to feel good all of the time. But that is not reality. And if we make pleasant emotions the number-one objective in life, our drive to serve those emotions will likely destroy us and all our relationships. *When emotions are lord, Jesus is not.* When emotions are lord, and when life gets difficult, we will see ourselves as a victim. The emotional victim assumes that he feels bad because of the behavior of others. Others are responsible for his ill feelings. Because others are responsible, he feels justified to manipulate and take advantage of others for his own emotional survival. He can even justify bitter hatred.

You may be thinking that you do not act out of your emotions as a victim. But have you ever been guilty of sulking? Have you ever had a hurtful dispute with your spouse and proceeded to be silent, turned off, and rejecting? When this occurs and evening comes, do you go to bed back-to-back—playing the victim role—waiting for your spouse to break down and say something? Do you lie there, unable to sleep as you mull over the events, making the offense greater and greater? Do you exaggerate your spouse's faults, making yourself a bigger and bigger victim?

Pain Can End in Victory

Some emotions are filled with pleasant and delightful feelings. We all want to feel joyful, content, hopeful, loved, appreciated, happy, valuable, and so on. No one likes feeling rejected, jealous, regretful, lonely, depressed, and the like. So what should we do when we suffer with ill feelings? What should our attitude reflect?

First, let it be said that it is not wrong to desire deliverance from emotional suffering. No one enjoys physical or emotional pain. We should be calling out to God in our struggles with pain and suffering. The Psalms clearly portray seeking God in our afflictions. Holiness is not just toughing it out. In fact, that could be construed as pride. When Jesus suffered, he poured out his struggles to his heavenly Father, and his Father sent angels to strengthen him (Luke 22:42–44; Matthew 26:38–43).

That being said, *the right attitude may deliver you from the ill feelings.* It is one thing to pour out our struggles to God with submission to his will. It was God's will that Jesus suffer. It may be God's will that you suffer. It is altogether different to allow our emotions to rule over our relationships with others and with God. Usually, our emotions follow a particular circumstance in our life. Let's say that you got fired from your job. There are all sorts of emotions that could result: rejection, anger, depression, fear, worry, shame, for example. As a victim, you could blame your employer. You could blame God for not protecting and providing for you, essentially implying that God does not love you. You could feel sorry for yourself. You could view yourself as deserving entitlements from the government in the form of unemployment benefits, food cards, or even disability payments. You may feel entitled to help from your church, relatives, and friends.

It is not wrong to receive help. What we're talking about is an attitude of being entitled to help because you are a victim. This attitude comes from a perception that is derived from your ill feelings. These feelings are derived from a victim perspective of your situation. All can change if you take on a victorious and redemptive view instead. *The right attitude may give you the strength and endurance to rise above your emotions. The right attitude comes from a right perspective. A right perspective comes from knowing how God sees your life.*

Most of our emotional pain in life is the result of personal interactions with people. We may feel the pain of being mistreated by others, or we feel cheated in life compared to the lives of others. We live in a fallen world of sin. Sin offends. Sin destroys. In the end, sin kills. As Christians, we have the victory, but how does this victory play out while we live in this fallen state?

Peter described what our attitude should be like as we live for Christ—as we suffer for him.

> Dear friends, do not be surprised at the painful trial you are suffering, as though something strange were happening to you. But rejoice that you participate in the sufferings of Christ, so that you may be overjoyed when his glory is revealed. If you are insulted because of the name of Christ, you are blessed, for the Spirit of glory and of God rests on you. If you suffer, it should not be as a murderer or thief or any other kind of criminal, or even as a meddler. However, if you suffer as a Christian, do not be ashamed, but praise God that you bear that name. (1 Peter 4:12–16 NIV)

Peter is talking about suffering as a Christian because you are a Christian, but the attitude is still applicable. James instructs us to have a positive view of suffering. Suffering may be unpleasant, but with the proper attitude, it will mold our character. It will strengthen our faith. It will drive us to spiritual maturity. It will make us more fruitful. A victim mentality of our emotional suffering will not produce good fruit, but a victor's mentality strengthens us and produces in us the likeness of Jesus, not lacking anything.

> Consider it pure joy, my brothers, whenever you face trials of many kinds, because you know that the testing of your faith develops perseverance. Perseverance must finish its work so that you may be mature and complete, not lacking anything. (James 1:2–4 NIV)

Paul understood rejection, misfortune, and hardship of many kinds. (Read 2 Corinthians 1:23–33.) Paul suffered pain at the hand of Satan by the will of God, and Paul accepted it with a positive attitude, knowing that God was developing his faith and character, even protecting him from a fall.

> To keep me from becoming conceited because of these surpass-ingly great revelations, there was given me a thorn in my flesh, a messenger of Satan, to torment me. Three times I pleaded with the Lord to take it away from me. But he said to me, "My grace is sufficient for you, for my power is made perfect in weakness." Therefore I will boast all the more gladly about my weaknesses, so that Christ's power may rest on me. That is why, for Christ's sake, I delight in weaknesses, in insults, in hardships, in persecutions, in difficulties. For when I am weak, then I am strong.
> (2 Corinthians 12:7–10 NIV)

Paul did not take on a victim attitude in his torments. He saw that his suffering made him strong in Jesus Christ. A victim attitude of our suffering will not make us strong in Christ. Instead, it will rob us of every spiritual blessing and in return, drive us toward defeat and a continual striving for deliverance and survival, but never reaching victory. Look at Paul's attitude as he wrote others from prison.

> I rejoice greatly in the Lord that at last you have renewed your concern for me. Indeed, you have been concerned, but you had no opportunity to show it. I am not saying this because I am in need, for I have learned to be content whatever the circumstances. I know what it is to be in need, and I know what it is to have plenty. I have learned the secret of being content in any and every situation, whether well fed or hungry, whether living in plenty or in want. I can do everything through him who gives me strength.
> (Philippians 4:10–13 NIV)

Contentment is a decisive attitude. Contentment is resting in God's choices for our lives. Contentment is resting in God's provision and bless-ings for the sake of living for his will first in our lives. Contentment is depending on God. We cannot be truly content without also having God's will as our focus. Paul wrote Timothy,

But godliness with contentment is great gain.
(1 Timothy 6:6 NIV)

A victor's attitude is "great gain." A victim's attitude is great loss.

Reflection Questions

When your spouse upsets you, how do you justify your hurt feelings? How do you portray yourself as the victim?

How do you view suffering?

How have you suffered emotionally? What has your attitude been?

How has your attitude produced gain or loss?

Where do you need to repent regarding your view and attitude toward your emotions?

Chapter 9

Self, the Greatest Enemy

The victim sees himself as the one who has been offended by others. Initially, that may be a proper perspective. But one who holds onto a victim view becomes his worst victimizer. His entire life becomes a trap, and he cannot escape. His viewpoint brings about depression, hopelessness, bitterness, anger, anxiety, and self-pity. He fails to have close relationships, because everyone becomes his enemy. Because of his constant complaining and blaming, no one wants to be his friend. He never experiences the joy of the Lord that comes by giving up his life for others (John 15). He may fail at his endeavors at work, at home, his relationships, and so on not because of others but because of his view of himself.

Labeled a Victim

Ben was raised in an abusive, dysfunctional home. His mother was angry and controlling. His father was a drunk and did not show love to his wife or children. Ben was exposed to physical abuse, emotional abuse, rejection, judgment, and distrust. He managed to grow up, go off to college, and break free from his home life. But no matter how far away he lived, he was not free. He carried around inside of him all of the pain, rejection, and distrust that was deeply planted in him as a kid.

All of his new relationships were tainted by his distrust of others. No matter who he was with, he was looking for a problem. He saw himself as a victim, so everyone was a potential victimizer. If someone asked him about what he did over the weekend, he assumed that they were looking for information to judge him and to spread a bad report to others. As a consequence, he did not inquire about what others did in their personal lives. He isolated himself, because he saw himself as a victim and everyone else as a potential enemy. His isolation was not physical; in other words, he was not a loner. He worked, joined a church, and engaged in group activities. But he was isolated, because he distrusted others without good reason. He was forever looking at others as potential perpetrators. The slightest infraction was construed as a deliberate infraction of privacy for the purpose of using it against him.

Consequently, he had few friends. And when he was around the few friends that he had, he constantly complained about how others were criticizing him, judging him, plotting against him, and doing things behind his back. Even his friends were not comfortable around him because of his constant complaining about others and his perpetual suspicions. There was no joy. Life was a continual struggle about others. And most of the time, the struggle was fueled by Ben's perfectionism, criticism, and distrust.

Employment became very difficult. He did not get socially close with any of his work associates, who worked as a united group. He did his job but was disconnected. He was always suspicious that his fellow workers were giving the supervisor a bad report about him. And occasionally they did. He became a target, because he placed himself on the outside.

To make it worse, Ben was a self-perceived perfectionist. Everything was to be done in a certain prescribed "right manner." "A good person and a good worker did everything to perfection—according to the rules." Self-worth was equated with perfection—obeying all the rules perfection. "How could anyone judge or criticize Ben if he was perfect?" Of course, no one is perfect, so this pursuit was like "chasing the carrot." One way to feel better about yourself if you are not perfect is to judge others when they fail to do everything just right according to the rules. And that is what Ben did.

Ben saw himself as a victim. In his never-ending striving to become perfect, he wore himself out, and the net result was not contentment, happiness, and high self-worth. Instead, he was continually faced with failure, which only made him feel worse. In all of his judgments, rejections, and isolationism, he had few friends, he did not enjoy his work, and he jeopardized his employment. He was fired from several jobs, not because he was irresponsible or because his work was substandard; quite the contrary. He got fired because he did not get along with fellow workers.

Even in his thirties, he was still trying to get the love and approval of his parents. He was captive. He thought that if he could just get them to affirm him as a good and successful person, he would be free from feeling like a victim. What he did not understand was that his parents were also captives. They, too, lived out their lives as victims. They were not about to change. And even if they did, Ben's true value was never based on what his parents thought of him. Ben did not see that escape from being a victim was within his own heart. Victimization was a perception that he owned.

Of course, children are supposed to be raised with loving and encouraging parents. But when that is not the case, we are not stuck in a state of self-worthlessness. We have a heavenly Father, and he is perfect at loving us. We were created by him for his purposes. As Christians, we have received his Spirit to live within us. We have the promise of inheriting his life in his kingdom and to live with him forever. We are everything in him and to him. We have nothing to fear.

But the self-proclaimed victim misses all of this. Oh, Ben was a Bible-reading Christian, and he professed all of these good things about himself. But he lived out a very different belief about himself. Ben was his greatest enemy. Ben was a victim of himself.

Harold is another self-victim. Harold is a failure at his work, a failure at having a disciplined life, a failure as a husband, and a failure as a parent. He fails but not because he does not have the potential of being successful. He fails because he has decided to proclaim himself a victim, so now he is not responsible to succeed. It is a deceptive form of irresponsible laziness.

Harold also came from a dysfunctional home. And like so many children today, he was labeled with a learning disability. It seems like everyone has a label today: ADD, ADHD, bipolar, PTSD, and so on. The *Diagnostic and Statistical Manual of Mental Disorders* lists over three hundred psychiatric disorders. This is not to imply that all of these psychological problems are not real. The caution is that we are quick to label people, and that label becomes an identity that may stay with the person and handicap him for the rest of his life. The label can be a disorder that overshadows the initial evaluation.

That was Harold's problem. He was labeled and drugged for his disorders throughout his childhood and on through his teen years. He claims that he was perpetually spaced out from the drugs and never lived a normal life like the rest of the kids. Harold was taken off these drugs when he became an adult, but labeling himself as a handicap remains. He proclaims to have sleep apnea. So he cannot stay awake to work, go back to school, or drive others (but he still drives for himself). He claims to be diagnosed with MS, but does not exhibit any physical impairments. Now he is classified as disabled, "can't work," and he receives a disability check from the government. Harold still works on his own car and does landscaping, carpentry, and all of the normal physical activities associated with work. But in Harold's mind, he is handicapped. Now he has an excuse: he is a victim. "He has been dealt a bad hand." "He has not been naturally blessed like most everyone else."

Harold is a proclaiming victim. He hangs onto these labels because they give him an excuse to fail, to be lazy, to be irresponsible, and to be at the mercy and care of society.

Our oldest son, Peter, did not begin to talk until he was three. He did not begin to read an entire book until he was ten. School was always difficult for him. We homeschooled our nine children. Compared to his siblings, learning clearly was a greater challenge. Fortunately for Peter, he did not go to public school as a youngster and, therefore, did not get a label from the institution. For sure he would have been enrolled in special education classes. He would not have been challenged, encouraged, and pushed to succeed. He would have been culturally labeled as "stupid." Instead, because he was homeschooled, we just told him that learning came harder for him and that he was going to have to work harder than others in order to learn. He understood that if he worked hard, he could learn like all of the rest. And that is what he did. To make a long story short, Peter graduated from college with bachelor's and master's degrees in mechanical engineering, and today, he has a thriving career in industry. I do not believe he would have succeeded if he had carried the labels that so many other kids carry because of their "learning disabilities."

Special Power from God

We have all been created in the image of God. Christians have an additional advantage; they have been born again by the Spirit of God. The all-powerful Spirit lives within every Christian, and he lives his life through our life. When we are weak, his strength shines through us. Paul knew this strength from God, which was revealed in Paul when he was weak.

But he said to me, "My grace is sufficient for you, for my power is made perfect in weakness." Therefore I will boast all the more gladly about my weaknesses, so that Christ's power may rest on me. That is why, for Christ's sake, I delight in weaknesses, in insults, in hardships, in persecutions, in difficulties. For when I am weak, then I am strong. (2 Corinthians 12:9–10 NIV)

The grace of God is the power of God within us to live a redeemed life so that God's will can be accomplished in and through us. Our strength is not our own; it is his.

I can do everything through him who gives me strength. (Philippians 4:13 NIV)

It would be easy to conclude that others are blessed but not me. In other words, "I am a victim. Others are not. Others have been loved; I have been unloved." When we profess these beliefs, we miss God. We miss out on his power working in our lives. He has given you life. He is still here to give you life. There is a saying, "God doesn't make junk." We are not a rejected mistake.

For you created my inmost being; you knit me together in my mother's womb. I praise you because I am fearfully and wonder-fully made; your works are wonderful, I know that full well. My frame was not hidden from you when I was made in the secret place. When I was woven together in the depths of the earth, your eyes saw my unformed body. All the days ordained for me were written in your book before one of them came to be. (Psalm 139:13–16 NIV)

He has a purpose for all of us. However, when we take on a victim mentality, we are not walking in his purposes. A life with Jesus is victorious. To be victorious, we need to take on some new labels, like "child of God" or "born again of his Spirit."

Refusing to Accept the Victim Label

Nick Vujicic was born without arms or legs. If anyone were justified to be angry with God and see himself as a victim, one would think it would be

Nick. But Nick is the exact opposite. His positive view of his life comes from his attitude. His positive attitude begins with seeing himself as a child of God. He is thankful for his life—the way it is, without arms and legs.

Nick travels around, giving motivational presentations to others with handicaps and people who have viewed themselves as unfortunate (victims). He speaks standing on a table. Since he doesn't have legs (just a couple little flippers where legs normally exist) standing is kind of a balancing act. He talks about getting up after falling down and then he suddenly falls over. But he doesn't stay down. He wiggles and contorts, and eventually, he is back up. And he is full of joy and thankfulness. Here are a few of Nick Vujicic's quotes.

I never met a bitter person who was thankful. Or a thankful person who was bitter.

It's a lie to think you're not good enough. It's a lie to think you're not worth anything.

In life you have a choice: bitter or better? Choose better; forget bitter.

If I fail, I try again, and again, and again.

Life without limbs? Or life without limits?

If you can't get a miracle, become one.

The challenges in our lives are there to *strengthen* our *convictions*. They are *not* there to run us over.

Obviously, Nick does not view himself as victim. If he had, he would not lead a victorious life today.

Joni Eareckson Tada was a beautiful seventeen-year-old when one day, she dove into shallow water and broke her neck. She became a quadriplegic. Now, at sixty, she suffers constant pain and is battling breast cancer. But she has not lost her joy, and she does not see herself as a victim. She is a powerful Christian woman who has availed her life to be used by Jesus Christ. In fact, God has used her handicap and suffering to draw her close to him and to equip her for his greater work. Her accomplishments outweigh most of us.

Joni is founder and chief executive officer of Joni and Friends International Disability Center and an international advocate for people with disabilities. She has written over forty books, recorded several musical albums, and starred in a major autobiographical movie of her life. She has learned to paint with a brush, using her teeth, and has sold her artwork.

She has received numerous awards and honors, including the American Academy of Achievement's Golden Plate Award, the Courage Award from the Courage Rehabilitation Center, the Award of Excellence from the Patricia Neal Rehabilitation Center, the Victory Award from the National Rehabilitation Hospital, and the Golden Word Award from the International Bible Society.

Joni does not view herself as a victim; she views herself as a child of God, created for his glory and purposes. She lives victoriously, in spite of her physical handicaps, pain, and battles for health.

Here are a few of Joni Eareckson Tada's quotes.

The best we can hope for in this life is a knothole peek at the shining realities ahead. Yet a glimpse is enough. It's enough to convince our hearts that whatever sufferings and sorrows currently assail us aren't worthy of comparison to that which waits over the horizon.

When I was on my feet, big boisterous pleasures provided only fleeting satisfaction. In a wheelchair, satisfaction settles in as I sit under an oak tree on a windy day and delight in the rustle of the leaves or sit by a fire and enjoy the soothing strains of a symphony. These smaller, less noisy pleasures are rich because, unlike the fun on my feet, these things yield patience, endurance, and a spirit of gratitude, all of which fits me further for eternity. It is this yieldedness that gains you the most here on earth.

Whatever troubles are weighing you down are not chains. They are featherweight when compared to the glory yet to come. With a sweep of a prayer and the praise of a child's heart, God can strip away any cobweb.

Even though I have rough moments in my wheelchair, for the most part I consider my paralysis a gift. Just as Jesus exchanged the meaning of the cross from a symbol of torture to one of hope and salvation, He gives me the grace to do the same with my chair. If a cross can become a blessing, so can a wheelchair. The wheelchair, in a sense, is behind me now. The despair is over. There are now other crosses to bear, other "wheelchairs" in my life to be exchanged into gifts.

It is a glorious thing to know that your Father God makes no mistakes in directing or permitting that which crosses the path of your life. It is the glory of God to conceal a matter. It is our glory to trust Him, no matter what.

David Ring was born in 1953 with cerebral palsy. He was orphaned at fourteen. His life has been one of physical struggles, struggles to talk, struggles to walk, struggles to use his hands. He has also experienced inner struggles of loneliness, hopelessness, and rejection. At seventeen, he gave his life to Christ, and Jesus gave his life to David. Since that time, David has not allowed his physical handicaps to handicap his life. He graduated from college. He is married with four children. And for decades, he has traveled around the country, giving motivational talks. He has availed himself to be used by God to bless others in their struggles. Here are few of David Ring's quotes.

I have cerebral palsy, but cerebral palsy don't have me.

If you don't like the way I am, hang in there. I'm still in the oven. God's still in the kitchen, and God's still cooking on me. And when God is finished cooking on me, God is going to pull me out of the oven, and God's going to say, "Well done, good and faithful servant."

God … why were you so good to me?

I have cerebral palsy and I serve the Lord with all that is within me; what's your excuse?

Don't be a "victim" … be a champion!

Living a life as a victim of any circumstance will rob anyone of a victorious life. When we define ourselves as a victim, we become a victim, not of others as much as a victim of our own making. True victory in life is all about our attitude. True victory comes through Jesus Christ. Without his life flowing through ours, we are all destined to lose. We can't blame others. It is our choice. Which one will you make?

Reflection Questions

What labels have been placed on you by society, others, or your circumstances? Which of these labels have you adopted as your identity?

What terrible things have happened to you? What terrible things are happening now in your life? How have they corrupted your attitude?

Do you believe that you "can do everything through Jesus who gives you strength" (Philippians 4:13)? Describe your relationship with him. How is he your life, your purpose, and your strength?

What describes you most: bitter and complaining or thankfulness and joy? Excuses and failures, or perseverance, faith, and success?

Chapter 10

Addictions and Destructive Behaviors

There is a huge irony—actually a tragedy—with many having a victim identity. They proceed through life perceiving a need to protect themselves from victimization. However, in their relentless pursuit for self-preservation, they often practice behaviors and make decisions that rob them of life.

For example, they may be oversensitive and perceive the tiniest infraction as a major offense, thereby alienating those they may desire for close friendship. They may become antisocial, never allowing themselves to trust others; so now they are without close friends. But the lack of close friends is misconstrued as rejection, which confirms the victim identity.

A marriage can be destroyed because the victim is forever accusing and treating the spouse as mistreating him or her. The victim may even be the one to file for divorce or separate because of the perceived need to protect oneself from further abuse. The abuse may have been as simple as not spending enough time together, not conceding to the victim's priorities, or not caring or loving enough. So now they are divorced, and they do not spend any time together. They have to share the kids. They both have to live on a tight budget, because they have two households to maintain, not to mention the huge lawyer fees incurred. They have to establish a new social life, because they no longer have a spouse to share life with. Life for the victim is filled with loss.

Victims are insecure and spend most of their energy attempting to be in control of their security. This is a hopeless pursuit. As a consequence, victims may pursue an addictive behavior as a means for being in control of their feelings, even if they cannot control their supposed safety from others.

All addictive behaviors have a common outcome. They produce brain chemicals to stimulate the pleasure center of the brain. Smoking, alcohol, drugs, overeating, workaholism, perfectionism, over-neatness, pornography, gambling, and so on may be practiced with the driving force of relieving the pain that comes from feeling like a victim and forever working to stand up for oneself. The addiction most likely does make them feel better while under the influence. But most addictions do not add to life; they destroy and rob us of life. In an effort to be in control, the addiction controls the user. So now, the victim becomes the victim of the addiction.

A victim may see himself as being cut short by society. He sees others as having all the right opportunities. And he sees himself as one of the unfortunate. He does not associate his lack of life's blessing to his lack of ambition and effort. Instead, he blames society. Maybe he sees others as being prejudiced because of his race or sex. So he blames his failures and lack of prosperity on society and does not see his lack of personal responsibility. In reality, he has been cut short, but not because of prejudice or ill favor of any kind. He came up short in life because he lived his life as a victim and not as a victor. As a victim, he never saw himself as being responsible for his own progression in life. It was always someone else's responsibility to promote him to better things. Again, he became a victim of his own mentality. The "victim" label became his excuse for failure, and so he failed—he failed himself.

Peggy is a middle-aged, married, and educated woman with three children. Her life is good, with much to be thankful for. One would think that her life should be filled with happiness and joy. But that is not the case for Peggy. She is rarely content, satisfied, or joyful. Her life is filled with disorder. She over-commits. Her house is stuffed and cluttered. And she complains about everyone. Someone has always been irresponsible and let her down. In reality, Peggy is the one who is normally irresponsible. She gets involved, commits to deadlines, and then frantically completes her commitments at the very last minute or too late. She holds up and frustrates all of the other team members. One would think that she would take personal responsibility, apologize, and become more responsible. That is not the case. She blames everyone else for holding her up. Or maybe she blames them for not informing her with the proper details, or for not getting things to her earlier. Peggy is a professing Christian, and she works with other Christian women who volunteer their time, talents, and energies. As Christian women, they make loving attempts to fill in where Peggy comes up short. They forgive and overlook her shortcomings. You might think that Peggy would be appreciative for the grace, mercy, and patience of her friends. Again, that is not the case. It is nearly impossible to work cooperatively with Peggy without being accused and attacked by her. You see, Peggy sees herself as a victim. Others are out to get her, cheat her, and reject her. Peggy is a very aggressive and controlling partner. She must have her way! There is no compromise. Everything must revolve around her will. Anyone who opposes her will is seen as personally attacking her. Peggy is not happy. Her marriage is in trouble. She does not have close friends. Her life is falling apart. She is a victim of herself.

Most divorces occur because one or both spouses have classified themselves as a victim. Divorce is construed as the only available choice to escape the abuse of the spouse. The ill effects of a divorce are rarely considered.

- A simple and expedient divorce will likely cost several thousand dollars each for the husband and the wife's lawyer fees. I know of a couple who were in court numerous times over a couple years before the final divorce was settled. Their combined lawyer fees were closer to $100,000. Not to mention the extreme anguish that each of them had to carry over the legal disputes.
- Your standard of living will likely decrease now that you will have to maintain two households.
- Your relationship does not end with divorce. You still have to share the children (and grandchildren). You still have to work through child support payments and alimony. You may not be able to move away from your spouse while the children are minors.
- Your children will no longer have the same relationship with you as when you were married. To them you are Dad and Mom. Now Dad and Mom reject each other for life. They are the true victims.
- Your children will have wounds and scars from your conflict, your lack of commitment and lack of love for one another.

- Divorced people typically have more health and psychological problems.[12]
- Divorce is extremely painful no matter what the relational problems that existed in the marriage.
- Divorced people are more likely to divorce again than those in first marriages.[3]

Victorious people pursue the problems in marriage. Jesus came to reconcile relationships. Sin is relational. Marriages fall apart because of sin. Jesus came to resolve our own personal sin issues. To run from marriage is to run from the work of Jesus within the husband and the wife—within the marriage.

Most victimization is relational. The victim in marriage is an obvious example, but like Peggy, all relationships are subject to viewing one's self as a victim. Victims run and lose. Victors stay and fight against the enemy of sin with the power of Christ. Our ultimate enemy is our own evil nature that lives within us and the Devil who is out to destroy us through deception and temptation. Jesus came so that we would not be their victims and would live victorious lives in righteousness and love.

Everyone who sins breaks the law; in fact, sin is lawlessness. But you know that he appeared so that he might take away our sins. And in him is no sin. No one who lives in him keeps on sinning. No one who continues to sin has either seen him or known him.

Dear children, do not let anyone lead you astray. He who does what is right is righteous, just as he is righteous. He who does what is sinful is of the devil, because the devil has been sinning from the beginning. The reason the Son of God appeared was to destroy the devil's work. No one who is born of God will continue to sin, because God's seed remains in him; he cannot go on sinning, because he has been born of God. This is how we know who the

---

1   Hughes, Mary Elizabeth, and Linda J. Waite. "Journal of Health and Social Behavior." *Journal of Health and Social Behavior*. 50.3 (2009): 344-358. Print. <http://hsb.sagepub. com/content/50/3/344.abstract>.

2   Lorenz, Frederick O., K. A. O. Wickrama, Rand D. Conger, and Glen H. Elder Jr. "Journal of Health and Social Behavior ." *Journal of Health and Social Behavior* . 47.2 (2006): 111-125. Print. <http://hsb.sagepub.com/content/47/2/111.abstract>.

3   Banschick, M.D., Mark. "The High Failure Rate of Second and Third Marriages." *Psychology Today*. Psychology Today, 06 2012. Web. 27 Oct 2012. <http://www. psychologytoday.com/blog/the-intelligent-divorce/201202/the-high-failure-rate-second-and-third-marriages>.

children of God are and who the children of the devil are: Anyone who does not do what is right is not a child of God; nor is anyone who does not love his brother.

This is the message you heard from the beginning: We should love one another. Do not be like Cain, who belonged to the evil one and murdered his brother. And why did he murder him? Because his own actions were evil and his brother's were righteous. Do not be surprised, my brothers, if the world hates you. We know that we have passed from death to life, because we love our brothers. Anyone who does not love remains in death. Anyone who hates his brother is a murderer, and you know that no murderer has eternal life in him.

This is how we know what love is: Jesus Christ laid down his life for us. And we ought to lay down our lives for our brothers. (1 John 3:4–16 (NIV)

Victims lose out in life because they live the role of victim. Since victimization is mostly a relational issue, victims ruin most of their relationships with complaining, accusing, attacking, and whining. They experience loneliness, depression, and isolation not because of others but because of their own inner struggles with others. Victims commonly find temporary escape in addictions, which robs them of even more life. In the end, they become a true victim of their own destructive behaviors.

Escape from this destructive behavior comes from the Savior. Jesus came to save us from our enemies (Luke 1:68–75), and much of the time our greatest enemy lies within us. Victims typically do not understand their own hearts. They do not see that they are the offensive one who needs a cure.

The heart is deceitful above all things and beyond cure. Who can understand it? (Jeremiah 17:9 NIV)

The victim looks at everyone else and believes that they are the ones who need to repent and change their ways. All along, they do not realize that repentance and healing must begin in their own heart. They are the ones in need of the Savior, the deliverer, or the healer.

For this people's heart has become calloused; they hardly hear with their ears, and they have closed their eyes. Otherwise they might see with their eyes, hear with their ears, understand with their hearts and turn, and I would heal them. (Matthew 13:15 NIV)

If you are a self-proclaiming victim, call out to Jesus to open your eyes and give you sight. Repent of your offensive and destructive behavior so that you may be healed—so that you may have true life and may be life to those around you, rather than the one who is ever complaining that you are the one who is not loved.

Reflection Questions

How have you perceived yourself as a victim? What does that look like in your relationships?

How have your relationships suffered because of your victim status and behavior?

How have you been your own worst enemy? How has being a victim ruined your life?

How have you medicated your ill feelings with an addiction? How has the addiction robbed you of life?

How do you need to repent of your self-justified offenses because you have seen yourself as the victim?

Chapter 11

I Am Entitled

We hear a lot about entitlements. To be entitled to something is to lay claim to a special right or privilege. It is to view access to a benefit as though it was owed to you. Entitlements include all of these indebted obligations. It is almost as though the recipient was receiving a paycheck for services rendered, but in the case of government entitlements, there are no reciprocal obligations. One just receives them because of their status (low-income, handicapped, unemployed, aged, unwed mother and so on).

Federal and state governments spend over $600 billion each year on welfare. This is money for child support, to help low-income families, and for worker's compensation, disability, food stamps, and so on. Should we be responsible for everyone's welfare? Are we helping or enabling people who are on these programs? Are we encouraging people to become dependent on government resources by allowing them, even encouraging them, to be classified as victims of society?

Biblical Basis

The Bible is clear that there are those who are poor and those who are rich, those who are weak and those who are strong. The Bible is also clear that the rich are to give to the poor, and the strong are to help the weak. God created humankind to live in loving unity. If we all looked after each other's needs, no one would go without. Some may have a little more than they need, which would provide the opportunity to give to the ones who do not have enough.

> Our desire is not that others might be relieved while you are hard pressed, but that there might be equality. At the present time your plenty will supply what they need, so that in turn their plenty will supply what you need. Then there will be equality, as it is written: "He who gathered much did not have too much, and he who gathered little did not have too little."
> (2 Corinthians 8:13–15 NIV)

It is not right for us to ignore those in need when we have what they need. It is not a matter of luxury. Rather, it is a matter of making sure that no one is without his or her basic needs, like food and clothing. James challenges us with the understanding that caring for one another is a demonstration of our faith in God.

> If a brother or sister is poorly clothed and lacking in daily food, and one of you says to them, "Go in peace, be warmed and filled," without giving them the things needed for the body, what good is that? (James 2:15–16 ESV)

John wrote that our love for one another is because we have received the Spirit of God. We are to love as Jesus loved us.

> This is how we know what love is: Jesus Christ laid down his life for us. And we ought to lay down our lives for our brothers. If anyone has material possessions and sees his brother in need but has no pity on him, how can the love of God be in him? Dear children, let us not love with words or tongue but with actions and in truth. (1 John 3:16–18 NIV)

Paul instructs the strong to help the weak, that we are to look after our neighbor for his good welfare in order to build him up.

> We who are strong ought to bear with the failings of the weak and not to please ourselves. Each of us should please his neighbor for his good, to build him up. (Romans 15:1–2 NIV)

And, of course, Jesus commanded us to "Love your neighbor as your-self" (Matthew 22:39).

This is not just a New Testament teaching. The Israelites were com-manded to give sacrificially to the poor and needy (Deuteronomy 15:7–11). They were to bring a tithe (10 percent of their income) to the leaders every three years in order to feed the priests, fatherless, and widows (Deuteronomy 14:28–29).

It should be obvious from these references that God's people have a responsibility to care for the poor and less fortunate.

Government Welfare

With these biblical mandates, it would seem appropriate that a Christian nation would have a thorough welfare system to take care of the unfor-tunate who live among us. Let's take a look at our system and how it has grown over the past half century.

President Lyndon Johnson promoted the ideal of the Great Society where we, as a nation, would advance a "War on Poverty". He made this announcement in his State of the Union address in 1964. What has this war cost America? And how successful have we conquered poverty in this expensive war? When launched, welfare spending was about $8.9 billion per year ($65 billion per year adjusted for inflation from 1964 to 2011). [1] Today we are spending about $1 trillion per year (not including social security and medicare).[2] That is a fifteen fold increase in constant dollars.

With all of these entitlements in our "War on Poverty", poverty has not been reduced. According the the US Bureau of Census, the portion of families below the poverty threshold was 15 percent in 1970 and was still at 15 percent in 2011. During these years, the actual number of Americans below the poverty level grew from 30.4 million to 46.2 million.

---

1   Robert Rector, "Means-Tested Welfare Spending: Past and Future Growth." *The Heritage Foundation*: *www.heritage.org/research/testimony/means-tested-welfare-spending-past-and-future-growth*. March 7, 2001 (January 20, 2012).

2   Rector, Robert, and Rachel Sheffield. "Welfare Spending at All-Time High...and Growing." *The Heritage Foundation*. The Heritage Foundation, 22 2012. Web. 28 Oct 2012. <http://www.heritage.org/research/commentary/2012/10/welfare-is-at-an-all-time-high>.

What Went Wrong? What Actually Happened?

What initially looked like a loving program to care for the weak and poor has actually been a driving force to motivate more and more Americans to engage in a government-supported life. Instead of motivating children and adults to become hardworking and self-sustaining, we have encouraged them to see themselves as needing special help, as underprivileged, as victims of circumstances—as victims. Numerous generations have grown up with their grandparents and parents dependent on government support. We are becoming a society with a victim identity, people who see themselves as entitled to be cared for by the government.

Our society has become one of entitlements. A large segment of our nation views itself as significantly disadvantaged compared to others. They have a victim view of themselves such that they perceive themselves as an unfortunate underdog. "Everyone else had all the lucky breaks." "Everyone else was given special advantage and privileges." They see government as the agency to stick up for them. They expect government to look after them by taking from the rich and giving it to the less fortunate—the victims.

Fred was a union worker in the automobile industry. At thirty-five, he hurt his neck when lifting a heavy object on the job. Now at forty, he is still off work, collecting disability pay. Fred manages to work on his car, complete yard work—including cutting down trees on his property with his chainsaw—and he keeps in shape on his weight machine in the garage. He maintains his disability designation because he has a medical report revealing spinal damage in his lower neck. Fred's wife works, and with his $1,000 per month government check for his "disability," they get by. Fred has filed a suit with the company where he got hurt. He hopes to get a $100,000 settlement.

Fred has classified himself as a victim. Considering all of his physical work around home, he obviously could work doing something. But Fred has evaluated his situation, and he thinks he is better off declaring himself a victim of his employer. Fred has not realized that he is a relatively young man without a purpose in life. His main focus has been to collect money for being injured on the job. He even complains about how he needs more and how he should get more. His life is at a dead-end. Fred is a victim. He is a victim of throwing his life away for the guarantee of being cared for by the government and his former employer for the rest of his life.

We have a responsibility to take care of the poor, the lame, and the aged, but what about Fred? Factually, Fred can work. He may not be capable of doing heavy lifting, like he did in his old job, but he is not incapable of becoming a valuable, contributing member of society.

How does this compare with the previous biblical commands to care for the weak and the poor? Paul instructed us regarding aid to those who are capable of working.

> For even when we were with you, we gave you this rule: "If a man will not work, he shall not eat."
> We hear that some among you are idle. They are not busy; they are busybodies. Such people we command and urge in the Lord Jesus Christ to settle down and earn the bread they eat. And as for you, brothers, never tire of doing what is right.
> (2 Thessalonians 3:10–13 NIV)

Yvonne is twenty years old. She had her first child at fifteen. She now has three. She has never been married, and she has never had a steady job. She dropped out of high school. Yvonne receives food stamps, Medicaid, and child subsidies. She also gets a bag of groceries each week from a local food bank. Yvonne perceives her government checks as working people do their paycheck. She does not see the relationship between working at a job and receiving a paycheck for services rendered. She does not see that those who are employed have a huge portion of their check taken out to pay taxes to the government. The government then takes part of this tax money to create Yvonne's check. Yvonne does not contribute to providing for the basic needs of society. That is what people do who have a job. Yvonne does not have a job. She lives in Michigan and receives her check through the Family Independence Agency (FIA). She sees herself as being independent, because she lives in her own place, buys groceries, and pays bills like everyone else. But in reality, the FIA has made Yvonne more dependent. The agency has supported her view of herself as being needy and less fortunate, and needing to be supported through dependence on government programs.

Yvonne is a victim with no escape. She is not a victim because opportunities were unavailable. Yvonne is a victim, because she has chosen to live a victim's life. Her mode of caring for herself has been to get herself pregnant and have another child to increase her government support.

Harry had a job. He worked as a construction laborer. He averaged about $3,000 per month when employed. Harry likes being laid off for the winter months. He volunteers to be first on the layoff list. He earns nearly

$25,000 over the eight months of work. Now he receives a $1,500 a month government check while he is off work during the winter. Harry thinks this is great. He gets a four-month vacation at half pay. He is off all winter, so he bought a snowmobile to enjoy while he is home without work.

Construction is slow right now, and Harry may be out of work longer than four months, maybe eight to twelve months. His unemployment check runs out after six months. Harry complains a lot about how the government doesn't care for the "little guy." He challenges them with, "How am I going to take care of my family?" The government program offers up to $4,000 to retrain him for another line of work, but Harry says that nothing else fits his personality. He complains, "Why isn't the government doing something to stimulate the economy so that the construction work will start up again?" And, "How am I supposed to find a job when I can't afford to put gas in the car and pay my cell phone bill?" Harry used to smoke a pack a day, but with all the stress that he is under, he has increased his consumption to a pack and a half. And instead of having just a couple of beers a day, he now relaxes with a six-pack. He has a lot of friends who are "down and out," just like him. They have each other for support as they complain over a game of pool at the corner bar and consume a few beers, cigarettes, and maybe pizza for lunch.

Isn't Harry right? There are those who have high-level jobs and make five or ten times what Harry makes. And they wouldn't have their elaborate office buildings if not for the hardworking construction workers. Shouldn't Harry be compensated for his unfortunate circumstances?

What about blacks or women in the workplace? Shouldn't they get special preference? Isn't it true that they have been held back over the millenniums because of their race or sex? Aren't they entitled to preferred treatment to make up for being neglected in the past? Isn't it just and fair to have hiring and promotion quotas that favor blacks and women to ensure they are not being overlooked compared to white males? Aren't they entitled? Haven't they been the victims all these years?

It may be true that there has been prejudice and bias, but is that how you want the decisions to be made for your next job or next promotion? What if the white male is more skilled, more experienced, and has better character? Do you want the decision to favor you because of your minority status? If yes, do you feel entitled because you are a victim, and now it is the white male's turn to be the victim—even if he may be more qualified?

Aiding the Unfortunate with Discretion

Years ago we took in a destitute seventeen-year-old single mother of a new-born. Sharisha was a very intelligent young girl. She grew up in the city, in a culture of government dependency. Many young women like herself had children out-of-wedlock and were supporting themselves through the Michigan FIA. It was at Sharisha's request that we took her in as part of our family. We loved her and her baby, cared for them, and provided for them like members of our family. We got her started in a home business to provide some personal income as well as give her an appreciation for her contribution to others. One day I asked her what she would do if there were no limits. Without hesitation, she said, "Become an attorney." So we began looking into how she could fulfill her ambition. We agreed on becoming a paralegal as a short-term goal.

Sharisha was already receiving FIA aid. One day I drove her there for an appointment. She gave me permission to sit in with her and her caseworker. She was getting money for food, transportation, housing, and so on. I spoke up to inform the caseworker that those things were all being provided for her through living in my household. The caseworker instructed me to be quiet. Then the caseworker continued to add up all of the qualifying benefits. If she got a job away from home, they would even provide $1,200 for a car.

I thought, *These are my tax dollars she is giving away, and I am already providing for this young girl and her baby.* I was trying to lead her into having a self-sustaining and independent life. FIA was actually promoting long-term dependence on the government. Sharisha was already visualizing a real future for herself, and they were leading her in the other direction of lifelong dependence.

One day she was on the phone with a friend from the city. Her friend was also dependent on FIA handouts. Her friend wanted Sharisha to leave our home and come live with her. She argued that the two of them could do quite well by combining their incomes (government handouts). At first Sharisha argued that she was going to become a paralegal. However, they kept talking, and sometime in the night, her friend came to pick her up. Sharisha thought that by living apart from us, she was going to be in more control of her life. But from that point on, her life went downhill. She would have been much better off if FIA had wisely cut off her aid because she had the opportunity to live with us. She came to our home as a victim with a victim mentality, and she left because of it. She could have been victorious, but with the encouragement of government officials, she continued in her victim role.

Paul gave Timothy some godly advice for handling the aid to unfortunate widows. Paul is firm in his instructions. He does not condone supporting those who are capable. He also instructed Timothy not to support those who have not demonstrated hard work in the past. He was also concerned that if people are supported, they may become lazy and just hang out with others, polluting the environment with their talk. This example of how to treat widows can be expanded to cover most "unable to work" situations.

> Honor widows who are truly widows. But if a widow has children or grandchildren, let them first learn to show godliness to their own household and to make some return to their parents, for this is pleasing in the sight of God. She who is truly a widow, left all alone, has set her hope on God and continues in supplications and prayers night and day, but she who is self-indulgent is dead even while she lives. Command these things as well, so that they may be without reproach. But if anyone does not provide for his relatives, and especially for members of his household, he has denied the faith and is worse than an unbeliever.
>
> Let a widow be enrolled if she is not less than sixty years of age, having been the wife of one husband, and having a reputation for good works: if she has brought up children, has shown hospitality, has washed the feet of the saints, has cared for the afflicted, and has devoted herself to every good work. But refuse to enroll younger widows, for when their passions draw them away from Christ, they desire to marry and so incur condemnation for having abandoned their former faith. Besides that, they learn to be idlers, going about from house to house, and not only idlers, but also gossips and busybodies, saying what they should not. So I would have younger widows marry, bear children, manage their households, and give the adversary no occasion for slander. For some have already strayed after Satan. If any believing woman has relatives who are widows, let her care for them. Let the church not be burdened, so that it may care for those who are truly widows. (1 Timothy 5:3–16 ESV)

What can be concluded from Paul's instructions?

- Only help those who are truly in need, who cannot help themselves.
- Standards should be established for whom to help. For example, if they refuse to budget, refuse to refrain from expensive habits, refuse to eliminate the unnecessary, and refuse to change their lifestyle, refuse to help them.
- Help those who have a reputation of being productive.
- Families should care for each other before looking for help from non-family members.
- Do not enable a person to become lazy. Do not enable a lazy person.

Victim of Laziness

There are certainly people who are "down and out." These people should be helped. However, entitlements have crippled more people than they have helped. We have produced a culture of victimization. We have encouraged people to become victims. And they do become victims—victims of laziness, victims of a depraved view of their life, and victims of self-imposed failure.

Practicing an unproductive lifestyle and then living off of the prosperity of those who are productive is a legal form of theft. It thrives on the Robin Hood principle: steal from the rich and give to the poor. Our political process provides the mechanism for a modern-day Robin Hood. Those who view themselves as victims can vote for their representatives in government who will create programs to tax the working class in order to provide benefits to those who are not productive. As the numbers of the unproductive increase, the more political power they have to vote into office those who will support their self-serving cause.

Paul firmly instructed Christians to work to supply the needs of others rather than to put oneself on the receiving end.

He who has been stealing must steal no longer, but must work, doing something useful with his own hands, that he may have something to share with those in need. (Ephesians 4:28 NIV)

Paul wrote that we are to work without being dependent on anybody so that we "win the respect of outsiders." In other words, hard work and independence are godly characteristics, and laziness and dependence are ungodly and unattractive.

> Make it your ambition to lead a quiet life, to mind your own business and to work with your hands, just as we told you, so that your daily life may win the respect of outsiders and so that you will not be dependent on anybody. (1 Thessalonians 4:11–12 NIV)

We all should do everything that is within our capabilities to be productive and independent so as not to be an unnecessarily burden to others, the church or the government.

There will be some who are truly incapable of working to supply their own needs. We should provide for those who are truly less fortunate because of circumstances beyond their control.

For the rest of us, we should view ourselves are being created by God to prosper in our work and to be a blessing, not a burden. Those who see themselves as requiring the support of others are victims of forever being dependent and struggling to survive. They become lazy, but they cannot see that their poverty stems from their view of themselves, not from a lack of opportunity. Laziness is a curse!

> The sluggard's craving will be the death of him, because his hands refuse to work. All day long he craves for more, but the righteous give without sparing. (Proverbs 21:25–26 NIV)

The lazy are victims but not of society. They are the victims of not taking hold of their life and applying themselves. They reap poverty and become its victims.

> Go to the ant, you sluggard; consider its ways and be wise! It has no commander, no overseer or ruler, yet it stores its provisions in summer and gathers its food at harvest. How long will you lie there, you sluggard? When will you get up from your sleep? A little sleep, a little slumber, a little folding of the hands to rest—and poverty will come on you like a bandit and scarcity like an armed man. (Proverbs 6:6–11 NIV)

> I went past the field of the sluggard, past the vineyard of the man who lacks judgment; thorns had come up everywhere, the ground

was covered with weeds, and the stone wall was in ruins. I applied my heart to what I observed and learned a lesson from what I saw: A little sleep, a little slumber, a little folding of the hands to rest—and poverty will come on you like a bandit and scarcity like an armed man. (Proverbs 24:30–34 NIV)

Reflection Questions

Are you classified as disabled? What are you still capable of doing? How could you be a productive member of society?

Are you an unwed mother? How have you been irresponsible? How have you become a burden to society?

Were you a hardworking and good student? Have you graduated from high school? Do you have a college degree? What skills have you developed, and how are you using them to serve society?

Do you see yourself as a victim of society, deserving special treatment because of your status, gender, or race?

How are you a victim of your own view of yourself? How has your negative view of yourself become your curse and your biggest handicap?

Chapter 12

Somebody's Out to Get Us

Paranoia is a tendency toward excessive or irrational suspicion and distrust of others. It is always viewing others as plotting against you. This is especially true when dealing with people in authority or power, or having influence. The paranoid victim walks around in fear that they will be victimized anytime, so they must always be watching and putting up their guard against an unseen assailant.

On the larger scale, many believe that there are conspiracies contrived by people in high places to control mankind. There are hundreds of these theories out in the media with large followings of those who believe they are true. Here are just a few examples.

AIDS is a man-made disease, created by the African governments as a means of population control to weaken racial minority groups and gay people. Some also say that there is a cure for AIDS being held back by the government for similar reasons.

The US government was involved in 9/11. They believe that George W. Bush and company wanted to gain more power quickly and get the support of the people. It's been said that the World Trade Center towers came down as a result of planted explosives, and a plane didn't crash into the Pentagon.

Auto companies have conspired with the world's oil producers to maintain low gas mileage and high consumption. They have secretly withheld special carburetor technology that would allow all of us to get one hundred miles per gallon.

Pharmaceutical companies, along with the rest of the medical industry, have found cures for various diseases, but they are holding them back so that they can profit through expensive drugs and medical procedures by keeping us sick.

How can people ascribe to such theories? People who see themselves as the targeted victim of those in power will believe whatever supports their victimized view of themselves as compared to the perpetrators, those deemed to be in control. Jesus commanded and encouraged us many times not to fear. But a victim makes a personal choice to suspiciously walk in fear and distrust.

Tony is a thirty-six-year-old African American. Like most people, He struggles with his job performance and recognition. Tony sees his white counterparts getting promotions ahead of him. He is convinced that it is because of his race. Prejudice against African Americans has been a serious offense and still exists. However, one with a victim identity may see most shortcomings as coming from prejudice, even when race is not the issue.

Tony grew up poor in the city. Actually, Tony has advanced further than his brothers, cousins, and childhood friends. Most of them did not even graduate from high school. But Tony not only graduated from high school, he got special training in the US Air Force. He is now an aircraft equipment repairman. Tony grew up knowing prejudice. He saw that blacks lived in rundown neighborhoods in the city, while whites lived in big new houses in the suburbs. Blacks drove old cars, while the whites purchased new ones. He sees that since the days of slavery, the black man has always gotten second-best, or worse. Tony does not see all of the whites who are not being promoted. In fact, most employees do not get promoted; there are only so many spots at the top. Most work in the middle of the pack. But Tony is convinced that someone has it out for him. He sees himself as a designated victim of prejudice. It is a conspiracy to advance whites and to hold blacks back.

Tony is not the only victim. Glenn has been in and out of prison several times in his twenty-eight years of life. Even as a teenager, it seems like he was always in a juvenile detention facility. He wondered, *Why has someone always been against me?* He thought the cops had it in for him and that they always had their eye on him, looking for the slightest slipup. The judge was no better in Glenn's view. "Just the way he would look at me or talk to me, I knew he had it in for me. I'm not a bad person, but there is a plot to put me away. The cops, the judges—they're all evil. I'll never trust them. I have to fend for myself."

Glenn is not the only one who thinks this way. Have you ever been at the mercy of a judge? If it did not work out in your favor, what did you conclude about the judge and his or her motives? Are judges, or a particular judge, your enemy? Are judges out to rob you of justice? If you have been through a divorce, how fairly were you treated by the judge? Have you deemed that your judge was biased and incompetent? Maybe you see yourself as a victim of those in power.

Driven by Fear

What drives people to be so suspicious of others, especially of those with power or influence? Obviously, we all struggle with perfection, and that includes everyone in an authoritative position. In fact, many in power are evil men with evil agendas. But that is not the issue here. The issue is viewing oneself as a victim such that we are forever suspicious of those in power, assuming they are evil and out to do harm.

How does someone become an overly suspicious victim? At some point in life, they may have been abused, neglected, ridiculed, shunned, or any number of things that made them a true victim of someone in authority. It could easily have been a domineering and unloving parent. So now the victim fears that there is always a hidden agenda. Therefore, they must always be on guard against a perpetrator lurking in darkness, hidden from sight. But you can see him! And it helps if others can see his evil plots with you. If others see him, too, the evil plots must be true. Thriving on conspiracies becomes an addiction based on inner distrust and fear.

> Do not call conspiracy everything that these people call conspiracy; do not fear what they fear, and do not dread it. The LORD Almighty is the one you are to regard as holy, he is the one you are to fear, he is the one you are to dread. (Isaiah 8:12–13 NIV)

Notice in these verses that there is a choice as to whom to fear. Either we can fear people and what they can do to us, or we can fear God. God can love and protect us, or he can bring about hardship and even cast our soul into hell. Jesus instructed his followers not to be afraid of those who plotted against them but to trust in God, who is in control of all things and the ultimate fate of all people.

> Do not be afraid of them, for nothing is hidden that will not be revealed, and nothing is secret that will not be made known. What I say to you in the dark, tell in the light, and what is whispered in your ear, proclaim from the housetops. Do not be afraid of those who kill the body but cannot kill the soul. Instead, fear the one who is able to destroy both soul and body in hell. Aren't two sparrows sold for a penny? Yet not one of them falls to the ground apart from your Father's will. Even all the hairs on your head are numbered. So do not be afraid; you are more valuable than many sparrows. (Matthew 10:26–31 NET)

Suspicious fear is a sign that we are not depending on God for our security. The Psalms are filled with proclamations that God is our refuge and strength against our enemies, and that we have nothing to fear. Here are just a few examples:

> I lie down and sleep; I wake again because the LORD sustains me. I am not afraid of the thousands of people who have taken their stand against me on every side.
>   Rise up, LORD! Save me, my God! You strike all my enemies on the cheek; You break the teeth of the wicked. Salvation belongs to the LORD; may Your blessing be on Your people. (Psalm 3:5–8 HCSB)

> The LORD delivers and vindicates me! I fear no one! The LORD protects my life! I am afraid of no one! When evil men attack me to devour my flesh, when my adversaries and enemies attack me, they stumble and fall. Even when an army is deployed against me, I do not fear. Even when war is imminent, I remain confident. (Psalm 27:1–3 NET)

God is our strong refuge; he is truly our helper in times of trouble. For this reason we do not fear when the earth shakes, and the mountains tumble into the depths of the sea, when its waves crash and foam, and the mountains shake before the surging sea. (Psalm 46:1–3 NET)

Even though I walk through the valley of the shadow of death, I will fear no evil, for you are with me; your rod and your staff, they comfort me. (Psalm 23:4 ESV)

Dwelling on the conspiracies of men with an inner drive to believe that their plots against man are true is a sign of not dwelling on the goodness and power of God.

The Devil Is a Conspirator

Is this to say that there are no conspiracies? Absolutely not. The world is filled with evil people. There are all sorts of evil agendas. Politics is driven by agendas, misrepresentations, brainwashing, and manipulation. We would be ignorant and naive to believe that every person can be trusted or his word with no evil intent.

Likewise, just as there are evil people who cannot be trusted, the one with a fearful victim mentality seeks to find an evil plot lurking in darkness. They are quick to believe an accusation, even when the accusation is false. Somehow they find security in finding those in power as being corrupt, untruthful, and plotting an evil agenda in secret.

Obviously, Jesus did not have an evil agenda. He came in love. He healed the sick and even brought the dead back to life. He spoke truth about all things. Those in power, the "church leaders" of the day, accused him of being an imposter with an evil plot to subvert the church and nation. They falsely accused him and convinced the people of his day that he must be crucified. They produced false witnesses against Jesus (Matthew 26:59–61; Mark 14:56). Before Pilate, they accused him of being a criminal with many false accusations (John 18:30; Mark 15:3). They paid one of Jesus' disciples (Judas) to betray him so that he could be arrested. There was definitely a conspiracy against Jesus.

Then the chief priests and the elders of the people assembled in the palace of the high priest, whose name was Caiaphas, and they plotted to arrest Jesus in some sly way and kill him. (Matthew 26:3–4 NIV)

Notice that the chief priests and the elders plotted against Jesus in a "sly way." They were planning a conspiracy against Jesus to make him out to be a conspirator. The irony is that the real conspirators were the accusers. Even though Jesus went about teaching love, performing miracles, healing thousands, and proclaiming the truth, the people were easily brainwashed into thinking this was an evil man who needed to be put to death. When before Pilate, the people cried out in unison, "Crucify him."

The question for today is, Who are the real conspirators? Jesus called the Devil the father of all lies. And he told the ones who were conspiring against him that the Devil was their father.

Jesus said to them, "If God were your Father, you would love Me, because I came from God and I am here. For I didn't come on My own, but He sent Me. Why don't you understand what I say? Because you cannot listen to My word. You are of your father the Devil, and you want to carry out your father's desires. He was a murderer from the beginning and has not stood in the truth, because there is no truth in him. When he tells a lie, he speaks from his own nature, because he is a liar and the father of liars. Yet because I tell the truth, you do not believe Me. Who among you can convict Me of sin? If I tell the truth, why don't you believe Me? The one who is from God listens to God's words. This is why you don't listen, because you are not from God."
(John 8:42–47 HCSB)

There is a real conspiracy and a real conspirator. The Devil works in darkness, and he is out to get us. He is the one who calls those who are good as being evil. He is continually plotting against God and God's people. He is continually leading us into false accusations and divisions. He is out to devour us.

Be sober and alert. Your enemy the devil, like a roaring lion, is on the prowl looking for someone to devour. Resist him, strong in your faith, because you know that your brothers and sisters throughout the world are enduring the same kinds of suffering.
(1 Peter 5:8–9 NET)

The Devil wants us to accuse others, but he is the one to accuse. Our ultimate battle is not against others, even if Satan uses them to fulfill his agenda.

Finally, be strong in the Lord and in his mighty power. Put on the full armor of God so that you can take your stand against the devil's schemes. For our struggle is not against flesh and blood, but against the rulers, against the authorities, against the powers of this dark world and against the spiritual forces of evil in the heavenly realms. Therefore put on the full armor of God, so that when the day of evil comes, you may be able to stand your ground, and after you have done everything, to stand.

In addition to all this, take up the shield of faith, with which you can extinguish all the flaming arrows of the evil one. (Ephesians 6:10–13, 16 NIV)

The Devil is a liar, a deceiver, and a conspirator. He is called the tempter. The whole world is under his control, and he leads the whole world astray (1 John 5:19; Revelation 12:7–9). He is the deceiver of the nations (Revelation 20:7–8).

What is his main conspiracy? The Devil deceived Eve by convincing her that she was better off being independent of God. In fact, he convinced her that God had deceived her, and as a consequence, she was cheating herself. In other words, there is a better life apart from God. In truth, there is no life apart from God. In essence, that is why sin results in death (James 1:13–15). All of his conspiracies stem from this main conspiracy. The Devil is out to pervert all of God's creation though deceptive lies. We trade God for money (Matthew 6:24). Men worship what God has created rather than the Creator. Men and women worship and degrade sex rather than the union of marriage (Romans 1:24–25). The wicked do not fear and trust God.

In his pride the wicked does not seek him; in all his thoughts there is no room for God. (Psalm 10:4 NIV)

Imagine this deception: "no room for God." God is the source of all of life, yet man has been deceived into thinking and acting as though he can produce life all on his own. He has been deceived into thinking that his own wisdom is sufficient.

Where is the wise man? Where is the scholar? Where is the philosopher of this age? Has not God made foolish the wisdom of the world? (1 Corinthians 1:20 NIV)

> For the foolishness of God is wiser than man's wisdom, and the
> weakness of God is stronger than man's strength.
> (1 Corinthians 1:25 NIV)

Yes, we were all victims of the Devil's deceptions. The Devil is a conspirator who works in darkness. But we do not have to live in darkness any longer. We no longer need to be his victims. Jesus came to destroy the Devil's work. He came as a light that shines on all of the Devil's hidden agendas. We just need to come out of the Devil's darkness and walk in Jesus' light, for his light exposes the deeds of darkness (Ephesians 5:13–14). To live in the light is to repent of living in the ways of darkness under the Devil's deceptions. We no longer have to live as a victim of the Devil; we can live victoriously in righteousness.

> Dear children, do not let anyone lead you astray. He who does
> what is right is righteous, just as he is righteous. He who does what
> is sinful is of the devil, because the devil has been sinning from
> the beginning. The reason the Son of God appeared was to destroy
> the devil's work. No one who is born of God will continue to sin,
> because God's seed remains in him; he cannot go on sinning,
> because he has been born of God. This is how we know who the
> children of God are and who the children of the devil are: Anyone
> who does not do what is right is not a child of God; nor is anyone
> who does not love his brother. (1 John 3:7–10 NIV)

The Devil may be the chief conspirator, but he has been found out and exposed. We just need to turn from living in his darkness according to the Devil's ways and begin to live in the light according to God's ways. This is called repentance. Repentance is the pursuit of eternal life. It is submitting to the Spirit as Jesus leads our lives. It is the pursuit of righteous living. It is the pursuit of living in the truth about all things rather than falling to the deceptive leadings of the Devil and the world in which he rules.

> Those who oppose him he must gently instruct, in the hope that
> God will grant them repentance leading them to a knowledge of
> the truth, and that they will come to their senses and escape from
> the trap of the devil, who has taken them captive to do his will.
> (2 Timothy 2:25–26 NIV)

We can choose life over death.

This day I call heaven and earth as witnesses against you that I have set before you life and death, blessings and curses. Now choose life, so that you and your children may live and that you may love the LORD your God, listen to his voice, and hold fast to him. For the LORD is your life. (Deuteronomy 30:19–20 NIV)

We can choose not to follow the Devil, to flee from him and temptations. We can choose to submit to God.

Submit yourselves, then, to God. Resist the devil, and he will flee from you. (James 4:7 NIV)

Yes, the Devil is out to get us, but we no longer have to live the life of a victim. A conspiracy loses its power when the lights are turned on to expose the evil plot. Jesus is our light.

When Jesus spoke again to the people, he said, "I am the light of the world. Whoever follows me will never walk in darkness, but will have the light of life." (John 8:12 NIV)

I have come into the world as a light, so that no one who believes in me should stay in darkness. (John 12:46 NIV)

Reflection Questions

Do you find yourself searching out conspiracy theories? Why do you thrive on them?

Do you typically hold people in authority as having a hidden agenda? Do you commonly suspect that they hold to a special interest group that excludes you? Describe your suspicions in detail.

Do you fear that those in authority are secretly plotting against you? Whom do you fear most and why?

How is the Devil behind the perversions of our cultural? Describe a specific perversion and how he has manipulated an influence. How has he remained hidden?

How has the Devil impacted your life? What damage has he done? How have you been deceived?

Have you come into the light of Jesus Christ? How have you repented in full knowledge of your destructive past? What do you see now that was not apparent before?

Chapter 13

The Walls of Isolation

Sara is a thirty-six-year-old married woman with several children. She has struggled being sexually intimate with her husband for their twelve years of marriage. She doesn't even want to hug or hold hands. She says that she just isn't that type of a person. Her husband, Greg, has been gentle and kind, but he struggles with the constant rejection.

Sara seems to be sociable, but she is always in control of the interactions. In fact, she dominates conversations. If she is involved in a Bible study, her remarks are purely factual; she does not share her personal feelings. On the contrary, she maintains a superior attitude so that she is not put on the spot to reveal any inward struggles.

Greg would like to have more intimate conversations with Sara, but she immediately criticizes and judges him about his behavior, character, thinking, decisions, and relationship with God. Sara is always in control. Greg has invited her to several support and accountability study groups with other men and women, but Sara always has an excuse to avoid attending. Sara did agree to seek marriage counseling, but after several sessions, it was quite clear that Sara did not think she was the problem in the marriage; Greg was the one who needed to change his behavior. Actually, Sara's main complaint was that Greg would not do things her way. She felt that the marriage would be just fine if Greg would fall in line and just listen and obey her demands.

Sara has no close friends. She has associations, but there is no one in her life whom she trusts. On an emotional level, she has no one to share her inner, personal struggles. She keeps it all to herself. On the outside, Sara seems confident, strong, and in control. On the inside, she is hurting, afraid, weak, and fearful of losing control.

Very few people know that Sara was born out-of-wedlock. She never knew her real father. He left when she was an infant. Her mother married another man when Sara was about five. Her stepfather was an angry man who physically abused her mother and sexually abused Sara. No one ever knew. On Sundays, they went to church. Her father was even an elder in the church. His homelife was never discovered. Everyone commented on what a great man he was. As a child, Sara had no place to run. Even her mother denied that there was a problem. Sara was trapped.

Sara has been out of her parents' home for eighteen years, but she is still trapped. She continues to see her parents, and she tells others that she had a wonderful family. She even tells herself. Sara lives in a world of her own. At a first meeting with her, one would think that she is a joyful woman with her life in control. But maintaining control is her wall that isolates her from all others. She lives in fear. She sees herself as a potential victim of everyone. She trusts no one, so she has developed a barrier to keep everyone at a distance so that they cannot hurt her. Her walls are superiority, criticism, control, domination, and avoidance. Inside she is very lonely, struggling, and confused. She is afraid to seek help, because in order to call out for help she would have to make herself vulnerable—she would have to trust another person with her true self. She cannot go there. She fears that she might become a victim.

Escape from a Horrible Trap

The irony of Sara's situation is that she truly is a victim; she is a victim of herself, of her own fears. Isolation from truthful relationships is abuse of the worst kind. We were created by God to have relationships. We were created in the image of God by God. God is a relational being, and he created us to be like him, relational beings. We were created to need each other. To isolate ourselves out of the fear of being vulnerable is to cut ourselves off from our most basic emotional and spiritual needs. They are like food and water to our soul. We need a relationship with God and a relationship with each other. This is the essence of true life. Without these relationships, we wither and die inside.

Some isolated people think that they have relationships, but their relationships are outward, not inward. The ones who isolate do so in public by maintaining control so that they dominate the conversation or limit the conversation to surface discussions to avoid their true identity. These relationships are not intimate. They are not based on love. We should not be fooled into believing that we can be intimate with God, whom we can trust, but avoid intimacy with people. In fact, if we truly trust God, we will trust him with our people relationships. Even our relationship with God requires us to have loving relationships with one another.

> Dear friends, let us love one another, for love comes from God. Everyone who loves has been born of God and knows God. Whoever does not love does not know God, because God is love. This is how God showed his love among us: He sent his one and only Son into the world that we might live through him. This is love: not that we loved God, but that he loved us and sent his Son as an atoning sacrifice for our sins. Dear friends, since God so loved us, we also ought to love one another. No one has ever seen God; but if we love one another, God lives in us and his love is made complete in us. (1 John 4:7–12 NIV)

True fellowship with God requires having true fellowship with each other. When Adam and Eve disobeyed God's warning not to eat of the Tree of the Knowledge of Good and Evil, the first thing they did was to cover up their own nakedness so as to hide (isolate) from each other. Then they hid among the trees to hide (isolate) themselves from God. When they were confronted with their disobedience, they immediately blamed others for their disobedience (Genesis 3:6–13) Not only did they hide, but when they were discovered, they hid themselves in a lie.

True fellowship with God requires us to come out of hiding, to come out into his light, where all can be seen not just by God but by each other. If we want to have fellowship with God, we must also have open fellowship with others. Isolation from others produces isolation from God as well.

> Now this is the message we have heard from Him and declare to you: God is light, and there is absolutely no darkness in Him. If we say, "We have fellowship with Him," yet we walk in darkness, we are lying and are not practicing the truth. But if we walk in the light as He Himself is in the light, we have fellowship with

one another, and the blood of Jesus His Son cleanses us from all sin. (1 John 1:5–7 HCSB)

If we are hiding from one another, we are also hiding from God. Adam and Eve hid from each other and from God out of shame and fear. The antidote for shame and fear is to trust God with our lives. To trust in God is pure wisdom. Trusting in our own ability to protect ourselves is pure foolishness.

The one who trusts in his own heart is a fool, but the one who walks in wisdom will escape. (Proverbs 28:26 NET)

He who trusts in himself is a fool, but he who walks in wisdom is kept safe. (Proverbs 28:26 NIV)

Trusting in God for our security is wisdom. God loves us and promises to protect us, even from those who may desire to harm us.

When I am afraid, I will trust in you. In God, whose word I praise, in God I trust; I will not be afraid. What can mortal man do to me? (Psalm 56:3–4 NIV)

To you, O LORD, I lift up my soul; in you I trust, O my God. Do not let me be put to shame, nor let my enemies triumph over me. No one whose hope is in you will ever be put to shame, but they will be put to shame who are treacherous without excuse. (Psalm 25:1–3 NIV)

We live in a very frightening world. Someone may physically abuse us, take from us, and worst of all, attack our character, self-worth, identity, and reputation. They may withhold love from us, judge us, criticize us, and slander our reputation with lies. It is understandable how someone who has been deeply hurt goes into hiding and is afraid to come out. It is understandable how they may be sociable on the outside, but no one ever sees the true inside. Someone may even be a very successful person in the world's eyes, but inside is trapped in fear, a lack of confidence, maybe even guilt and low self-worth. Those who have constructed these walls of isolation struggle with inner safety from those on the outside, but inside, they struggle with themselves. And there is no wall to protect us from the destruction that can occur all on its own within the heart of humans.

We have to make openings in these walls. The openings are decisive areas of trust. First, we trust God to love and protect us from all harm. We trust him to uphold us, even if we are under abusive attack. Then we openly choose to trust another individual. Trusting people is always a risk, as everyone struggles with their own sin, which has the power to offend. So how can we put ourselves at risk? Love is our shield and our weapon against evil. We are not to fear others; rather, we are to overcome the evil of others with the love of God.

Bless those who persecute you, bless and do not curse. (Romans 12:14 NET)

Do not be overcome by evil, but overcome evil with good. (Romans 12:21 NET)

This is how we should act in the presence of real enemies. Most isolation walls out everyone, even those we should trust. As Christians, we are to walk in the light, love, and power of God. We have nothing to fear. To love requires us to make ourselves vulnerable to being hurt. How else can we love our enemies (Matthew 5:43–48)? People who love us have significant power to enable us to come out of hiding. But no one will love us in perfection. Everyone has the potential to offend or hurt us. If we ever expect to be free from the walls of isolation that we have constructed, we will have to choose to tear them down. Removing stones from our walls is an act of love. It is an act of becoming vulnerable to others for the sake of having a relationship, because when isolated, we do not have true relationships. Love trusts in God first and then trusts in others, even if they are not fully trustworthy. God is fully trustworthy, and we love in trust because we put our security in the hands of God, who loves us without judgment. True love does not require a guarantee of love in return; it lives in the hope of better relationships, even if there is a struggle at present. True love presses ahead for the sake of love. It endures hardship and does not expect a safe journey or a blessing. True love perseveres for Christ's sake, that his kingdom may come and his glory seen. True love sacrifices of ourselves, even our security.

Love bears all things, believes all things, hopes all things, endures all things. (1 Corinthians 13:7 ESV)

It always protects, always trusts, always hopes, always perseveres. (1 Corinthians 13:7 NIV)

Tearing down our walls of isolation is a personal choice. It is a choice to come out of hiding. It is a choice to release our inner self from a dark bondage. It is a choice to serve Jesus. It is a choice to love. It is a choice to become vulnerable. It is a choice to advance an assault against the powers of darkness in a very dark world. It is a choice to be set free through the power of Jesus Christ.

Reflection Questions

How have you isolated your inner self from others?

Do you act social and outgoing on the outside but avoid any intimate contact where you reveal what really goes on deep inside—your fears, anxieties, and pains?

Are you free to give yourself to your spouse—emotionally, verbally expressing your thoughts, and physically with touch such as hugs and kissing? Do you withhold sexual involvement from your spouse?

Do you withhold trust out of fear of being hurt?

Has your isolation truly protected you, or have you developed more pain inside due to your self-inflicted isolation?

Are you willing to come out of your dark place and out into the light of Christ? Can you trust God with yourself? Can you begin to trust others, knowing that Jesus and your heavenly Father love you, protect you, and are with you in all situations and circumstances?

Are you willing to love by trusting your spouse and a few chosen friends? Are you willing to take the first steps of removing a few stones from your protective wall?

Chapter 14

Poor, Miserable Sinner
or Victorious Christian

Why was Jesus sent? That's a big question. I think most would say, "To die for our sins so that we could go to heaven, rather than hell." Is that it? Is that all that we find in Scripture? Are we just poor, miserable sinners in despair, waiting until the day when we die so we can go to heaven? Are we victims of this miserable life with no way out until death takes us away?

To answer these questions, let's take a look from God's perspective, answering what God is doing for himself through Jesus Christ.

The Establishment of God's Kingdom

Jesus came to establish his kingdom. Jesus is the King, and we are his subjects. He taught us to pray, "Your kingdom come, Your will be done on earth as it is in heaven" (Matthew 6:10). Notice that he said "on earth"; that means now, in this life. He told us to "seek first his kingdom and righteousness" (Matthew 6:33). Again, we seek them now in the life we live today. He said that his kingdom was good news, and that the good news of his kingdom would be told to all nations before the end would come (Matthew 24:14). He said that the reason he was sent was to proclaim the good news of the kingdom of God (Luke 4:43). He told us to store up treasures in heaven through our life here on this earth (Matthew 6:19–21). This life is filled with purpose. Jesus died to "purchase men for God" for his kingdom. He died to establish his kingdom, and we are the subjects of his kingdom. This begins now, in this life. He told us that his kingdom is in our midst (Luke 10:9–10; 17:20–21). That's pretty good news—for today and for eternity. We have a glorious future that begins now.

> And they sang a new song: "You are worthy to take the scroll and to open its seals, because you were slain, and with your blood you purchased men for God from every tribe and language and people and nation. You have made them to be a kingdom and priests to serve our God, and they will reign on the earth."
> (Revelation 5:9–10 NIV)

The blood of Jesus was shed to "purchase men for God," men and women for his kingdom. His blood was shed to free us from sin, not just to avoid the punishment for our sin. We are to be free from sin so that we can become the righteous subjects of his kingdom.

> Jesus Christ, who is the faithful witness, the firstborn from the dead, and the ruler of the kings of the earth. To him who loves us and has freed us from our sins by his blood, and has made us to be a kingdom and priests to serve his God and Father—to him be glory and power for ever and ever! Amen.
> (Revelation 1:5–6 NIV)

The grace of God is much more than forgiveness of sins, as essential as that may be. The grace of God is the power of God living and active in our lives so that we can live godly lives for the sake of Jesus and his kingdom.

> For the grace of God that brings salvation has appeared to all men. It teaches us to say "No" to ungodliness and worldly passions, and to live self-controlled, upright and godly lives in this present age, while we wait for the blessed hope—the glorious appearing of our great God and Savior, Jesus Christ, who gave himself for us to redeem us from all wickedness and to purify for himself a people that are his very own, eager to do what is good.
> (Titus 2:11–14 NIV)

Jesus came to buy us back from a life of wickedness (redemption) so that we could live a purified life of righteousness. He did this to "purify for himself *a people of his very own*, eager to do what is good." For we are destined to become the subjects of his kingdom. We are Jesus' precious people—now! We are no longer victims of sin and depravity.

God Is Building His House

We live in houses, but does God live in a house? Well, according to God, *we* are his house.

> But Christ is faithful as a son over God's house. And we are his house, if we hold on to our courage and the hope of which we boast. (Hebrews 3:6 NIV)

We are so special in God's sight! He is building a house for himself, and we are his living building materials. He will live with us, and we will live with him forever. He is forming his house, his dwelling place, now. He has already sent his Spirit to live within each one of us. He lives within every born-again Christian now. And he is remodeling each one of us into a gorgeous mansion as we unite together.

> As you come to him, the living Stone—rejected by men but chosen by God and precious to him—you also, like living stones, are being built into a spiritual house to be a holy priesthood, offering spiritual sacrifices acceptable to God through Jesus Christ. (1 Peter 2:4–5 NIV)

God does not live in a house made by man. All of man's houses are made of nonliving materials. God's house is alive. Jesus came so that we could be fully alive. That is why we have been given his Spirit to live within us. In fact, that is how God lives within his house, by his Spirit.

> Consequently, you are no longer foreigners and aliens, but fellow citizens with God's people and members of God's household, built on the foundation of the apostles and prophets, with Christ Jesus himself as the chief cornerstone. In him the whole building is joined together and rises to become a holy temple in the Lord.

And in him you too are being built together to become a dwelling in which God lives by his Spirit. (Ephesians 2:19–22 NIV)

That ought to make us feel pretty good. This certainly is not the life or the future of a victim. We are loved by God, and we are chosen by him to become his eternal, living house.

Family of God

We all know the desire—the necessity—to belong to a family. Our earthly families are a creation of God. Unfortunately, many of our families are filled with sin. All sin is relational. We sin against someone. Too many families today are filled with anger, violence, abuse, abandonment, selfishness, divorce, and so on. But that is not how they were meant to be. God intended them to be a place of things such as love, security, unity, caring, encouragement, belonging, identity, provision, purpose, personal growth, and support. Families are a place for a husband and wife to unite in love. Families are a place for brothers and sisters and a dad and mom. But sin has taken a horrible toll on marriages, families, and children. Far too many children today are not even born into a family. According to the US Department of Health and Human Services, over 40 percent of children are born to unmarried mothers. And according to the US Census Bureau for every two marriages, there is one divorce.

God understands the family; he created it. And he cares about the family. He cares for marriages and for children who grow up without fathers. God hates divorce (Malachi 2:16), And his heart goes out to children without fathers (Psalm 68:5–6; James 1:27; Exodus 22:22–23).

God also has a family of his own. That is why he is called our heavenly Father, and why we are called his children.

How great is the love the Father has lavished on us, that we should be called children of God! And that is what we are! The reason the world does not know us is that it did not know him. Dear friends, now we are children of God, and what we will be has not yet been made known. But we know that when he appears, we shall be like him, for we shall see him as he is. Everyone who has this hope in him purifies himself, just as he is pure. (1 John 3:1–3 NIV)

We are his children now. God is our Father now. We belong to his family now. We are not orphans, lost in this dark place. We are cherished by the Creator of the universe, and he is our heavenly Father, and we are his loved children. Like every good father, our heavenly Father is molding and shaping us into the glorious likeness of his Son Jesus. This is our hope now and forever.

God is our Father today, not just later, after we die. Like any good father, God the Father is training, teaching, molding, and shaping us now. He is making us into something great and beautiful. We are his kids!

> Endure hardship as discipline; God is treating you as sons. For what son is not disciplined by his father? If you are not disciplined (and everyone undergoes discipline), then you are illegitimate children and not true sons. Moreover, we have all had human fathers who disciplined us and we respected them for it. How much more should we submit to the Father of our spirits and live! Our fathers disciplined us for a little while as they thought best; but God disciplines us for our good, that we may share in his holiness. No discipline seems pleasant at the time, but painful. Later on, however, it produces a harvest of righteousness and peace for those who have been trained by it. (Hebrews 12:7–11 NIV)

Jesus is the Son of God, so we are brothers and sisters of Jesus. We are members together as part of God's family here on earth.

> For this reason I kneel before the Father, from whom his whole family in heaven and on earth derives its name.
> (Ephesians 3:14–15 NIV)

> Both the one who makes men holy and those who are made holy are of the same family. So Jesus is not ashamed to call them brothers. (Hebrews 2:11 NIV)

Many of us struggle with the hurt and rejection from our earthly families. But we have a heavenly family here on earth, the family of God. We can come together and live for one another as brothers and sisters of Jesus, having the same heavenly Father. We may have been victims of our earthly families, but now we belong to a victorious family of God.

Bride of Christ

Marriage is the closest, the most intimate relationship created by God on earth. When questioned, Jesus said that there would be no marriages between men and women in heaven (Matthew 22:23–30). Our earthly marriages are only for the present and do not carry on after death. However, our earthly marriages point ahead to the marriage between Christ and his Church, which does go on forever. Right now, we are engaged to be married to Jesus, the Son of God. All Christians united together become the bride of Jesus Christ. What a glorious place that we are destined to be the wife of the living God.

> Then I heard what sounded like a great multitude, like the roar of rushing waters and like loud peals of thunder, shouting: "Hallelujah! For our Lord God Almighty reigns. Let us rejoice and be glad and give him glory! For the wedding of the Lamb has come, and his bride has made herself ready. Fine linen, bright and clean, was given her to wear." (Fine linen stands for the righteous acts of the saints.) Then the angel said to me, "Write: 'Blessed are those who are invited to the wedding supper of the Lamb!'" And he added, "These are the true words of God."
> (Revelation 19:6–9 NIV)

We are not victims in God's eyes. We are engaged to become married to his one and only Son. Notice that "Fine linen, bright and clean was given her to wear" and that the "fine linen stands for the righteous acts of the saints." We are preparing for the wedding here and now by putting on the wedding clothes. We are making ourselves ready for him—for that glorious wedding day. The wedding clothes have been given to us by God, and now we can put them on.

> You were taught, with regard to your former way of life, to put off your old self, which is being corrupted by its deceitful desires; to be made new in the attitude of your minds; and to put on the new self, created to be like God in true righteousness and holiness.
> (Ephesians 4:22–24 NIV)

> Do not lie to each other, since you have taken off your old self with its practices and have put on the new self, which is being renewed in knowledge in the image of its Creator.
> (Colossians 3:9–10 NIV)

What bride is not anxiously waiting for the glorious day of her wedding? She spends all of her thought and time preparing for that marvelous day. We are the bride of Christ. We don't have a reason to see ourselves as victims any longer, because we are no longer victims! We have nothing but goodness and glory in our paths. We are becoming the righteousness of God (2 Corinthians 5:21).

Transformation

Christianity is not about joining a church or going to meetings, even though there is great value in being together to love and encourage one another (Hebrews 10:24–25). Christianity is all about transformation. We are being transformed into the image of Christ. Sin is killing us (James 1:13–15). But God loves us. He is transforming us from our state of sin, which is death, to a state of the glory of Jesus Christ, where there is true life. He sent his own Spirit to live within us to do this miraculous, marvelous work of life.

> Now the Lord is the Spirit, and where the Spirit of the Lord is, there is freedom. And we, who with unveiled faces all reflect the Lord's glory, are being transformed into his likeness with ever-increasing glory, which comes from the Lord, who is the Spirit. (2 Corinthians 3:17–18 NIV)

We are transformed by what and how we think. God has given us his living written word so that we can know good versus evil, right versus wrong, life versus death. As our thinking is transformed, we see and understand God more and more.

> Do not conform any longer to the pattern of this world, but be transformed by the renewing of your mind. Then you will be able to test and approve what God's will is—his good, pleasing and perfect will. (Romans 12:2 NIV)

Sin is death and captivity. Jesus came to release us from the bondage of sin so that we would be free and have life, his life.

> Just as you used to offer the parts of your body in slavery to impurity and to ever-increasing wickedness, so now offer them

in slavery to righteousness leading to holiness. When you were slaves to sin, you were free from the control of righteousness. What benefit did you reap at that time from the things you are now ashamed of? Those things result in death! But now that you have been set free from sin and have become slaves to God, the benefit you reap leads to holiness, and the result is eternal life. For the wages of sin is death, but the gift of God is eternal life in Christ Jesus our Lord. (Romans 6:19–23 NIV)

"The wages of sin is death." This is not a judgment; this is a consequence. Adam and Eve were warned not to eat of the Tree of the Knowledge of Good and Evil," for if they did, they would die. In other words, this knowledge would kill them. Sin kills. Jesus came to set us free from the sin that is killing us.

Jesus is without sin; he is eternal life. Jesus came so that we could become just like him and live forever. He came so that we would be transformed into his likeness. In this life, we are being transformed piece by piece. Some day all of his children will see Jesus face to face and be transformed in an instant into his likeness. This is our eternal hope: to become just like Jesus in his holiness. This is the promise of God, who loves those who are his. For now, we strive to know Jesus and become like him in his perfection. Our hope is in the day that we become completely like him. This hope to be like Jesus keeps us pure in God's sight.

Dear friends, now we are children of God, and what we will be has not yet been made known. But we know that when he appears, we shall be like him, for we shall see him as he is. Everyone who has this hope in him purifies himself, just as he is pure.
(1 John 3:2–3 NIV)

We are not poor, miserable sinners waiting to die. We are rich right now with the indwelling Holy Spirit and the Word of God. We are being transformed by God himself. We will inherit the kingdom of God and eternal life through Jesus Christ. We will be married to Jesus for eternity.

The Power of the Resurrection

I have attended many Good Friday and Easter Sunday church services over the years. It is wonderful to celebrate what Jesus accomplished by his death on the cross. That is Friday's message. Jesus paid the penalty for our sin on the cross.

> For the wages of sin is death, but the gift of God is eternal life in Christ Jesus our Lord. (Romans 6:23 NIV)

If we stop there, we are still captive and lost in our sin. "The wages of sin is death" is not God's judgment for our sin. That statement is the reality of the consequence of sin. Sin kills. If we sin, we are planting the seeds of sin. When sin is full grown, we die (James 1:13–15).

We are born into sin. We are born as victims of a deadly spiritual disease—sin! Jesus came so that we would be victorious over this internal enemy. On Good Friday we celebrate Jesus' death, which atoned for our sins and paid the price for our forgiveness. With forgiveness, our relationship with God is reconciled. Now that we are reconciled, God sends his Holy Spirit to live within us so that we have his nature and his power living to give us victory over our sinful nature that is killing us.

This is the message of Easter Sunday. Good Friday's message is the atonement by the death of Jesus. But that is not Easter Sunday's message. The Easter message is the resurrection of Jesus. What would have been accomplished on the cross if Jesus died but never rose from the dead? Jesus' resurrection is just as essential as his death. When Jesus rose and ascended to his heavenly Father, he sent back to us his own Spirit to reside within us. The power of Jesus' resurrection is the same power that gives us power over sin. We are no longer "poor, miserable sinners."

> And if the Spirit of him who raised Jesus from the dead is living in you, he who raised Christ from the dead will also give life to your mortal bodies through his Spirit, who lives in you.
> (Romans 8:11 NIV)

These are Paul's words in Romans 8. The chapter preceding is frequently misquoted. In chapter 7, Paul gives a dissertation of what it was like before he had any power over his sinful nature—when he was under the law and still a victim to the powers of death living within him. In his words, "I am unspiritual, sold as a slave to sin" (7:14). But Paul clearly stated in the preceding chapter, chapter 6, that we are no longer slaves to sin.

What shall we say, then? Shall we go on sinning so that grace may increase? By no means! We died to sin; how can we live in it any longer? Or don't you know that all of us who were baptized into Christ Jesus were baptized into his death? We were therefore buried with him through baptism into death in order that, just as Christ was raised from the dead through the glory of the Father, we too may live a new life.

If we have been united with him like this in his death, we will certainly also be united with him in his resurrection. For we know that our old self was crucified with him so that the body of sin might be done away with, that we should no longer be slaves to sin—because anyone who has died has been freed from sin.

Now if we died with Christ, we believe that we will also live with him. For we know that since Christ was raised from the dead, he cannot die again; death no longer has mastery over him. The death he died, he died to sin once for all; but the life he lives, he lives to God.

In the same way, count yourselves dead to sin but alive to God in Christ Jesus. Therefore do not let sin reign in your mortal body so that you obey its evil desires. Do not offer the parts of your body to sin, as instruments of wickedness, but rather offer yourselves to God, as those who have been brought from death to life; and offer the parts of your body to him as instruments of righteousness. For sin shall not be your master, because you are not under law, but under grace.

What then? Shall we sin because we are not under law but under grace? By no means! Don't you know that when you offer yourselves to someone to obey him as slaves, you are slaves to the one whom you obey—whether you are slaves to sin, which leads to death, or to obedience, which leads to righteousness? But thanks be to God that, though you used to be slaves to sin, you wholeheartedly obeyed the form of teaching to which you were entrusted. You have been set free from sin and have become slaves to righteousness.

I put this in human terms because you are weak in your natural selves. Just as you used to offer the parts of your body in slavery to impurity and to ever-increasing wickedness, so now offer them in slavery to righteousness leading to holiness. When you were slaves to sin, you were free from the control of righteousness.

What benefit did you reap at that time from the things you are now ashamed of? Those things result in death! But now that you have been set free from sin and have become slaves to God, the benefit you reap leads to holiness, and the result is eternal life. For the wages of sin is death, but the gift of God is eternal life in Christ Jesus our Lord. (Romans 6:1–23 NIV)

Paul may have been a "poor, miserable sinner" before receiving the Spirit of Christ, but by the power of Christ's resurrection, he walked victoriously over his sinful nature. Jesus set him free. He was no longer a slave to sin but a slave to righteousness. This is true for all who come to Christ and are born again of his Spirit, who then lives within us.

Following chapter 7, Paul goes on to tell about the power we have by the Spirit that lives within us, the Spirit that would not be available to us if it were not for Jesus' death *and* resurrection.

Therefore, there is now no condemnation for those who are in Christ Jesus, because through Christ Jesus the law of the Spirit of life set me free from the law of sin and death. For what the law was powerless to do in that it was weakened by the sinful nature, God did by sending his own Son in the likeness of sinful man to be a sin offering. And so he condemned sin in sinful man, in order that the righteous requirements of the law might be fully met in us, who do not live according to the sinful nature but according to the Spirit.

Those who live according to the sinful nature have their minds set on what that nature desires; but those who live in accordance with the Spirit have their minds set on what the Spirit desires. The mind of sinful man is death, but the mind controlled by the Spirit is life and peace; the sinful mind is hostile to God. It does not submit to God's law, nor can it do so. Those controlled by the sinful nature cannot please God.

You, however, are controlled not by the sinful nature but by the Spirit, if the Spirit of God lives in you. And if anyone does not have the Spirit of Christ, he does not belong to Christ. But if Christ is in you, your body is dead because of sin, yet your spirit is alive because of righteousness. And if the Spirit of him who raised Jesus from the dead is living in you, he who raised Christ from the dead will also give life to your mortal bodies through his Spirit, who lives in you.

Therefore, brothers, we have an obligation—but it is not to the sinful nature, to live according to it. For if you live according to the sinful nature, you will die; but if by the Spirit you put to death the misdeeds of the body, you will live, because those who are led by the Spirit of God are sons of God. For you did not receive a spirit that makes you a slave again to fear, but you received the Spirit of sonship. And by him we cry, *"Abba,* Father." The Spirit himself testifies with our spirit that we are God's children. (Romans 8:1–16 NIV)

The only poor, miserable sinners are those who see themselves as victims of sin with no power over sin. Sin destroys life. Jesus came that we would have life. He came that we would have victory over the Devil, over the world, and over our sinful nature. Those who belong to Christ live in these victories. Those who do not belong to Christ are still in bondage to all three. They are victims!

Everyone who sins breaks the law; in fact, sin is lawlessness. But you know that he appeared so that he might take away our sins. And in him is no sin. No one who lives in him keeps on sinning. No one who continues to sin has either seen him or known him.

Dear children, do not let anyone lead you astray. He who does what is right is righteous, just as he is righteous. He who does what is sinful is of the devil, because the devil has been sinning from the beginning. The reason the Son of God appeared was to destroy the devil's work. No one who is born of God will continue to sin, because God's seed remains in him; he cannot go on sinning, because he has been born of God. This is how we know who the children of God are and who the children of the devil are: Anyone who does not do what is right is not a child of God; nor is anyone who does not love his brother. (1 John 3:4–10 NIV)

This is love for God: to obey his commands. And his commands are not burdensome, for everyone born of God overcomes the world. This is the victory that has overcome the world, even our faith. Who is it that overcomes the world? Only he who believes that Jesus is the Son of God. (1 John 5:3–5 NIV)

Many today deny the victories described in these passages. *The problem centers on proclaiming forgiveness through Jesus but denying the power that we have in him and through him.* They are like those whom Paul wrote to Timothy, "Having a form of godliness but denying its power. Have nothing to do with them" (2 Timothy 3:5 NIV). Proclaiming our depravity is not humility; it is a denial of truth. It denies the power and will of God for our lives. It denies the power of the resurrection of Jesus Christ. For we are no longer victims; we are conquerors through the love of God.

> No, in all these things we are more than conquerors through him who loved us. For I am convinced that neither death nor life, neither angels nor demons, neither the present nor the future, nor any powers, neither height nor depth, nor anything else in all creation, will be able to separate us from the love of God that is in Christ Jesus our Lord. (Romans 8:37–39 NIV)

Reflection Questions

As a Christian, what is your hope for this life? What is your eternal hope for yourself?

How are you being transformed? Describe the "old self" and the transformation that is occurring in the way you think, the way you live, and in your relationships with others.

Have you received the Holy Spirit? Describe his work in your life with specific examples of how he has changed you.

How has Jesus empowered you to escape from your old life in order to live a victorious life? How are you not a victim any longer?

Do you need to repent of a false confession of Jesus' work for you and of yourself as a victim?

Chapter 15

Without Hope,
There Is No Hope

Sally was sexually abused as a child. The wounds and scars to her heart are still evident more than forty years later. Her husband is unloving and verbally abusive. They were both in a car accident, and he is now disabled and completely dependent on others for care. Sally's twenty-eight-year-old son's marriage just fell apart, and he lost his job, so now he is living at home with Sally. Due to the accident, Sally has panic attacks and is afraid to drive on major highways away from home. Her doctor says she is suffering from post-traumatic stress disorder (PTSD). He prescribed several antidepressants and psychotic drugs, and psychological therapy.

Sally has been clinically classified as a victim. Obviously, her life is filled with burdens that have no readily apparent remedies. To her, life is filled with too many struggles, too many responsibilities, too many handicaps, too many worries, too many anxieties, too many decisions, and far too few answers. Sally feels like a hopeless victim of her circumstances, who is struggling against an emotional collapse. Her doctor and psychologist have told her to drop all responsibilities. She has been told that she is incapable of handling her life. In other words, she has been labeled an emotional cripple. The abuse, her failing marriage, her husband's disability, the burden of her adult son, and her panic attacks are not her greatest enemy. *Her loss of hope is at the heart of her depression.* Without hope, there is no hope. This is true for all of us. Without hope, there is no hope for living.

Everyone struggles with life to some degree. We all need hope. Without hope, we will perish in despair and depression.

> Hope deferred makes the heart sick, but a longing fulfilled is a tree of life. (Proverbs 13:12 NIV)

We were created by God with a need to be loved, a need to love, a need for purpose, and a need for hope. Hope sustains us during our trials and hardships. Hope delivers from depression. Hope gives us the inner power to strive forward. Hope is the motivation to escape. Hope enables. Hope is victory.

Whenever we perceive ourselves as a victim, we abandon hope. To hope is to pursue victory. To wallow in an attitude of being a victim is to reject all hope.

So where does hope come from? Is it just a matter of positive thinking? What if we are hoping in something that will never deliver? What if the burdens of life do not subside?

Resting in the Love of Our Heavenly Father

When a young child struggles—assuming he has loving parents—he seeks out his dad or mom for help. Children do not normally carry the burdens of life; they rest in the security of their home. Dad and Mom carry his burdens. A child does not worry about paying bills, having food to eat, having a house to live in, or clothes to wear. When he is sick, Dad and Mom take care of him and, if necessary, take him to the doctor. Transportation is provided. Dad and Mom carry the responsibilities for his life. As a child, he can rest in the protection, care, and nurturance of his parents.

But what happens when the child grows up and is now responsible for his own protection and care, and possibly that of his own children and elderly parents? Like Sally, what if the burdens of life are too much to handle? We can't just revert back to our childhood days under the care of Dad and Mom.

Jesus taught us to pray, "Our Father who is in heaven." "Our Father!" We will always remain children in the eyes of God. He covers his children with his love. In God's family, we do not grow up and leave home.

How great is the love the Father has lavished on us, that we should be called children of God! And that is what we are!
(1 John 3:1 NIV)

We may be grown up and no longer live under our parents' provision and protection, but we are still children of the Most High God. And that will never change. The struggles and burdens that life can bring may not go away, but we can find rest for our soul in God. Hope comes from him, because he is above all our earthly struggles.

Find rest, O my soul, in God alone; my hope comes from him. He alone is my rock and my salvation; he is my fortress, I will not be shaken. My salvation and my honor depend on God; he is my mighty rock, my refuge. Trust in him at all times, O people; pour out your hearts to him, for God is our refuge.
(Psalm 62:5–8 NIV)

The young child does not collapse in despair, because he can depend on his parents to carry his burden. He still has needs and struggles, but his parents are there for him. God is always there for us—if we put our hope in him.

Why are you downcast, O my soul? Why so disturbed within me? Put your hope in God, for I will yet praise him, my Savior and my God. (Psalm 42:11 NIV)

In the midst of our struggles, we do not have to become a victim. In the midst of our struggles, we can be victorious conquerors through the loving and all-powerful hand of God. This is our hope in the face of life's trials and tribulations.

No, in all these things we are more than conquerors through him who loved us. (Romans 8:37 NIV)

As a child of God, we call out to our heavenly Father. He hears our cries for help, and he comes to our aid and support. Out of his love, he desires to come to our aid when distressed. He wants to support us and grant us the desires of our hearts so that we will succeed in life. He wants us to be victorious.

May the LORD answer you when you are in distress; may the name of the God of Jacob protect you. May he send you help from the sanctuary and grant you support from Zion. May he remember all your sacrifices and accept your burnt offerings. May he give you the desire of your heart and make all your plans succeed. We will shout for joy when you are victorious and will lift up our banners in the name of our God. May the LORD grant all your requests. Now I know that the LORD saves his anointed; he answers him from his holy heaven with the saving power of his right hand. Some trust in chariots and some in horses, but we trust in the name of the LORD our God. They are brought to their knees and fall, but we rise up and stand firm. O LORD, save the king! Answer us when we call! (Psalm 20:1–9 NIV)

The focus of our hope is on God's power and his faithfulness. Ultimately, everything comes from God. When Jesus' disciples asked him to teach them how to pray, he gave them what we call the Lord's Prayer. He taught them to ask for daily food and daily protection. In reality, we are totally dependent on God for everything. All life comes from God. He even gives us the air we breathe. Without rain, we would not eat. Despair and depression come from depending on everything except God. And when these things let us down, when life becomes too difficult for us to handle, we feel lost and hopeless. The answer for all our needs has always been the same—God! Not just when life is too difficult but for every tiny aspect of life. Our dependence on God is 100 percent for 100 percent of our life.

Blessed is he whose help is the God of Jacob, whose hope is in the LORD his God, the Maker of heaven and earth, the sea, and everything in them—the LORD, who remains faithful forever. He upholds the cause of the oppressed and gives food to the hungry. The LORD sets prisoners free, the LORD gives sight to the blind, the LORD lifts up those who are bowed down, the LORD loves the righteous. The LORD watches over the alien and sustains the fatherless and the widow, but he frustrates the ways of the wicked. The LORD reigns forever, your God, O Zion, for all generations. Praise the LORD. (Psalm 146:5–10 NIV)

Learning to Rest

Psalm 20:7 says, "Some trust in chariots and some in horses." Today we might say that some trust in money, their intellect, or their job title, or their social status. This list may incorporate any number of things that depend on our strengths. Our own strength may seem to work for a while, but in the end, it will fail us. The only true strength that does not fail us is God's. He is the only true hope.

We all strive to survive, to keep our lives afloat. For many of us our attempts to survive fail us and we may feel like our life is falling apart. We may have felt victorious at one time, but now we see ourselves as a sinking victim of this life's hardships. We may even call out to God for help, but his help does not seem to come. Now what?

Jesus certainly knows our painful struggle. He was born in a barn to a poor family. Since Jesus' birth, King Herod was out to kill him. His family had to flee to Egypt until Herod died. At thirty, Jesus called his disciples and began his ministry. He had no money. He was homeless. The leaders of the Jews were constantly plotting against him and attacking him. Eventually, they tortured and killed him. Even his own disciples abandoned him during his most intense suffering and trials. Jesus carried the sins and failings of every man and woman who will ever live. He definitely knows every one of our struggles!

In all of Jesus' struggles, he rested in the power and strength of his heavenly Father. He may be the Son of God, but he is also the Son of Man. He lived out his life on earth with the same frailties as every one of us. Yet, he was victorious in all of his painful trials. His own power and strength as a man would have failed him, but his heavenly Father did not fail him, even though he was subjected to severe hardships.

Jesus implores each one of us to come to him so that he can teach us to rest.

> Come to me, all you who are weary and burdened, and I will give you rest. Take my yoke upon you and learn from me, for I am gentle and humble in heart, and you will find rest for your souls. For my yoke is easy and my burden is light.
> (Matthew 11:28–30 NIV)

Notice in his words that Jesus says to take "my yoke upon you." A yoke is a bar or frame of wood by which two oxen are joined at the heads or necks for working together when plowing a field or pulling a cart. Jesus did not say that he would take our yoke upon him, rather that we are to take his yoke upon us. In other words, Jesus is not promising to come into our lives and help us carry all of the loads that we have chosen to drag along in life. Instead, he instructs us to take off our yoke that is too difficult to pull, and to come over into his field, take on his yoke, and pull alongside of him. Not only will he pull alongside of us, he said that his yoke is easy and that his burden is light. He said that he is gentle and humble, and if we will work alongside of him, he would teach us how to find rest for our souls.

How does this work? How can we find rest for our souls in the midst of our earthly trials? How can a wife find victorious rest in her marriage as she lives with an unloving husband? How can we find rest when we have lost our job and cannot pay the bills? How can we maintain our joy when the health of our body has failed us? How can we maintain our victory when our relationships are under attack, and we feel the pain of rejection and bitterness? How can we fail and yet remain victorious?

In our own strength, we cannot; victory is beyond our own powers. Many try, and many fail. After we fail many times, we give up in despair. No, true lasting victory only comes by the power of God working in our lives. And victory does not necessitate that all of our circumstances change. Victory is a spiritual work in our hearts and minds. Peace, joy, happiness, contentment, and hope are inner qualities that supersede all outward circumstances. Man typically tries to solve his problems in reverse. He works to change the outward circumstances in order to feel good on the inside. This approach never brings lasting satisfaction. It becomes an endless pursuit, where victory is always a little way past where we are presently. Truthfully, contentment, happiness, peace, and joy begin on the inside and permeate all our outward circumstances whatever they are, even pain and suffering.

Where does this inner peace—this inner power or strength—come from? It does not come from us; we do not conjure it up on our own resolve. This inner strength comes from God. It is available to everyone, but not everyone receives it. There is an imposing force against this peace and strength from God. The imposing force is the pride of our own hearts that lack faith in God. Instead of seeking God, we seek to resolve our problems in our own strength and powers, which are insufficient and incomparable to the power of God. Yet, in our foolish pride, we continue to rely on our own abilities. And when our own abilities run out and come up short of sustaining us, we slink into despair and depression without hope. Even then, we may not seek God. We may cover up our pain with drugs, alcohol, or other addictions. We may even seek a drug prescription from our physician. But none of these drugs will solve the true problem that resides in our soul. They may give us some emotional relief, but down deep inside, we are not filled with hope.

The Witness of Paul's Hope and Strength

Jesus specifically called Paul to suffer for him as he spread the message of Jesus.

> This man is my chosen instrument to carry my name before the Gentiles and their kings and before the people of Israel. I will show him how much he must suffer for my name. (Acts 9:15–16 NIV)

Think about this; Jesus called Paul to go to work for him, and he would have to suffer in the process. That doesn't sound too encouraging! And Paul suffered greatly.

> I have worked much harder, been in prison more frequently, been flogged more severely, and been exposed to death again and again. Five times I received from the Jews the forty lashes minus one. Three times I was beaten with rods, once I was stoned, three times I was shipwrecked, I spent a night and a day in the open sea, I have been constantly on the move. I have been in danger from rivers, in danger from bandits, in danger from my own countrymen, in danger from Gentiles; in danger in the city, in danger in the country, in danger at sea; and in danger from false brothers. I have labored and toiled and have often gone without sleep; I have known hunger and thirst and have often gone without food; I have been cold and naked. Besides everything else, I face daily the pressure of my concern for all the churches. Who is weak, and I do not feel weak? Who is led into sin, and I do not inwardly burn?
>
> If I must boast, I will boast of the things that show my weakness. (2 Corinthians 11:23–30 NIV)

We complain about having a bad day or a bad week. These are the complaints of a victim. Paul was not a victim, and he did not view himself as a victim, in spite of his very difficult hardships. Even from the confines of prison, Paul rejoiced in what God was doing through him. He rejoiced that God had not left him.

> Now I want you to know, brothers, that what has happened to me has really served to advance the gospel. As a result, it has become clear throughout the whole palace guard and to everyone else that I am in chains for Christ. Because of my chains, most of the brothers in the Lord have been encouraged to speak the word of God more courageously and fearlessly. (Philippians 1:12–14 NIV)

The key to Paul's joy and encouragement was because he did not live for his own purposes; he lived for the purposes of God. He lived to serve Jesus, his Lord, Master, and Savior. This made all the difference, and it will make all the difference for each one of us. It doesn't mean that we will become traveling missionaries, like Paul. But if Paul's life for Jesus radiated throughout the whole palace guard while he was in prison, our lives can radiate through all of our associations. Think about all the people who witness your life—friends, relatives, work associates, your church, your community, and so on. Are you living for Jesus? Do those around you see the power of Jesus in you? Or do they see someone who is sinking in despair because he is alone in this world, without power or purpose of character and life? Paul radiated purpose and hope in Jesus Christ no matter what his circumstances, even from prison.

> But what does it matter? The important thing is that in every way, whether from false motives or true, Christ is preached. And because of this I rejoice. Yes, and I will continue to rejoice, for I know that through your prayers and the help given by the Spirit of Jesus Christ, what has happened to me will turn out for my deliverance. I eagerly expect and hope that I will in no way be ashamed, but will have sufficient courage so that now as always Christ will be exalted in my body, whether by life or by death. For to me, to live is Christ and to die is gain.
> (Philippians 1:18–21 NIV)

Paul rejoiced in all circumstances. Instead of becoming anxious, he prayed about his circumstances, and he thanked God for his life. God did not always deliver him from his hardships, but God did give him his peace, and he kept Paul's mind focused on Jesus and his purposes. This would not have been the case if Paul had not chosen to live for Jesus rather than himself. Those who live for Jesus are not victims, no matter what their circumstances. Their circumstances do not define their lives; Jesus does.

Paul instructed us from his imprisonment.

> Rejoice in the Lord always. I will say it again: Rejoice! Let your gentleness be evident to all. The Lord is near. Do not be anxious about anything, but in everything, by prayer and petition, with thanksgiving, present your requests to God. And the peace of God, which transcends all understanding, will guard your hearts and your minds in Christ Jesus. (Philippians 4:4–7 NIV)

Paul found contentment in all life circumstances. He did not determine to be content when life's trials were taken from him. He did not base his contentment upon having all of his needs met. His contentment came from living for Christ. And then, as an outcome of his determination to live for Jesus, he was content and strengthened through Christ.

> I am not saying this because I am in need, for I have learned to be content whatever the circumstances. I know what it is to be in need, and I know what it is to have plenty. I have learned the secret of being content in any and every situation, whether well fed or hungry, whether living in plenty or in want. I can do everything through him who gives me strength. (Philippians 4:11–13 NIV)

We would think that through all of Paul's hardships he would be humble, but that is not how God saw him. Paul was humble, but God had a great calling upon his life, and he had received great revelations from God. Paul was working directly for Jesus to establish his kingdom upon earth. God saw it necessary to allow Satan to torment his flesh to add to his humility.

> To keep me from becoming conceited because of these surpassingly great revelations, there was given me a thorn in my flesh, a messenger of Satan, to torment me. Three times I pleaded with the Lord to take it away from me. But he said to me, "My grace is sufficient for you, for my power is made perfect in weakness." Therefore I will boast all the more gladly about my weaknesses, so

that Christ's power may rest on me. That is why, for Christ's sake,
I delight in weaknesses, in insults, in hardships, in persecutions,
in difficulties. For when I am weak, then I am strong.
(2 Corinthians 12:7–10 NIV)

Paul boasted about his weaknesses so that Christ's power would rest on
him. This certainly does not sound like he saw himself as a victim. Victims
complain, blame, manipulate, get depressed, and sink. Paul was victorious
through Christ, because he lived his life for Christ's purposes. And as a
consequence, Jesus upheld him.

God is the God of hope. He fills us with joy and peace as we trust
in him and him alone, not others or our own strength. God gives us his
powerful Holy Spirit so that we will overflow with his hope.

May the God of hope fill you with all joy and peace as you trust
in him, so that you may overflow with hope by the power of the
Holy Spirit. (Romans 15:13 NIV)

Reflection Questions

Do you lack hope? Are you discouraged and depressed? Is your life filled
with frustration and pain, and you do not see a way of escape? Do you feel
like you are sinking?

Have you cried out to God to uphold you? Describe your faith and prayers
for God's strength?

Do you believe that God can uphold you without changing your circumstances? How have you thanked him for your life and his presence? How
can you become victorious instead of a victim without your circumstances
changing?

How are you living for God versus living for your own desires? How does
that change your outlook on life?

How have you given your life to God such that you are content with the
life he gave you?

Chapter 16

Victory in Jesus

Was Jesus a Victim?

The Pharisees, Sadducees, and teachers of the law plotted against Jesus in order to kill him. They attempted to trap him in his own words many times, but failed. Eventually, they made up lies about him in order to condemn him. They hired one of Jesus' own disciples to turn on him and reveal his whereabouts. When Jesus was arrested, his disciples fled from him. Jesus was slandered, ridiculed, whipped, beaten, tortured, and hung on a cross until he died. It sure appears that he was a victim. Was Jesus a victim? What would Jesus say? What did Jesus say? First, he laid down his life willingly out of obedience to his Father's will.

> The reason my Father loves me is that I lay down my life—only to take it up again. No one takes it from me, but I lay it down of my own accord. I have authority to lay it down and authority to take it up again. This command I received from my Father.
> (John 10:17–18 NIV)

At his arrest, his disciples drew their swords in order to oppose the attack, but Jesus was clearly capable of defending himself against a few Roman soldiers. He made a conscious choice to withhold any retaliation.

"Put your sword back in its place," Jesus said to him, "for all who draw the sword will die by the sword. Do you think I cannot call on my Father, and he will at once put at my disposal more than twelve legions of angels? But how then would the Scriptures be fulfilled that say it must happen in this way?"
(Matthew 26:52–54 NIV)

Even after being severely beaten and hung on a cross, Jesus was still more concerned about the welfare of the ones who rejected him and eventually took his life.

Jesus said, "Father, forgive them, for they do not know what they are doing." And they divided up his clothes by casting lots.
(Luke 23:34 NIV)

Jesus knew ahead of time what was going to happen to him, but he pursued his cross because he knew that victory over sin and the Devil would come through his sacrifice. *He told his followers about the impending trial. And then he told them to suffer in like manner so that they, too, would be victorious over sin and the Devil.*

And he said, "The Son of Man must suffer many things and be rejected by the elders, chief priests and teachers of the law, and he must be killed and on the third day be raised to life."
Then he said to them all: "If anyone would come after me, he must deny himself and take up his cross daily and follow me. For whoever wants to save his life will lose it, but whoever loses his life for me will save it. What good is it for a man to gain the whole world, and yet lose or forfeit his very self? (Luke 9:22–25 NIV)

This is the ultimate victory! Victims are forever trying to escape, even at a cost to others. But true victory comes from "taking up our cross" for the sake of Jesus' purposes in this world.

For to this you have been called, because Christ also suffered for you, leaving you an example, so that you might follow in his steps.
(1 Peter 2:21 ESV)

Not Forsaken

When Jesus hung on a cross, he called out, "My God, my God, why have you forsaken me?" (Matthew 27:46). The Son of God and Son of Man was left alone on the cross. Jesus paid the price for our reconciliation with God so that we will never be forsaken or left alone without him (Romans 5:11; 2 Corinthians 5:18–19). God promises never to leave us, forsake us, or abandon us. He always remains at our side to love, guide, and protect us.

> "I will never leave you and I will never abandon you." So we can say with confidence, "The Lord is my helper, and I will not be afraid. What can man do to me?" (Hebrews 13:5–6 NET)

It does not matter what has happened in the past. Jesus came for us here and now. Even if our father and mother have forsaken us, the Lord will never do so.

> Even if my father and mother abandoned me, the LORD would take me in. (Psalm 27:10 NET)

This does not mean that there is nothing in this world to attack us. But in this dark, offensive world, we have someone who is all-powerful and has come to our aid to set us free and bring us victory against all that opposes us.

> In my anguish I cried to the LORD, and he answered by setting me free. The LORD is with me; I will not be afraid. What can man do to me? The LORD is with me; he is my helper. I will look in triumph on my enemies. It is better to take refuge in the LORD than to trust in man. (Psalm 118:5–8 NIV)

It is one thing to think that God is distant, but he quickly comes to my aid. It is another to think that maybe God is always near to hear my cries for help. But he is even closer than that. The Spirit of Christ has come to reside deep within us, and he never leaves us for any reason. God cannot get any closer than that.

> To them God has chosen to make known among the Gentiles the glorious riches of this mystery, which is Christ in you, the hope of glory. (Colossians 1:27 NIV)

Outwardly, we may come under attack from those around us, even by those we should expect to be trusted. Our security and victory in this world does not come because we are promised never to suffer or come under attack. Our victory comes because we are loved by God Almighty. He has given us a promise to be with us in all trials. He also promises to raise us up with him on the last day. That is the day when we will be forever free of anything that could come against us. The love of God is our victory now. The love of God is our promise for all of eternity.

> And we know that for those who love God all things work together for good, for those who are called according to his purpose. For those whom he foreknew he also predestined to be conformed to the image of his Son, in order that he might be the firstborn among many brothers. And those whom he predestined he also called, and those whom he called he also justified, and those whom he justified he also glorified.
>
> What then shall we say to these things? If God is for us, who can be against us? He who did not spare his own Son but gave him up for us all, how will he not also with him graciously give us all things? Who shall bring any charge against God's elect? It is God who justifies. Who is to condemn? Christ Jesus is the one who died—more than that, who was raised—who is at the right hand of God, who indeed is interceding for us. Who shall separate us from the love of Christ? Shall tribulation, or distress, or persecution, or famine, or nakedness, or danger, or sword? As it is written,
>
>> For your sake we are being killed all the day long; we are regarded as sheep to be slaughtered.
>
> No, in all these things we are more than conquerors through him who loved us. For I am sure that neither death nor life, nor angels nor rulers, nor things present nor things to come, nor powers, nor height nor depth, nor anything else in all creation, will be able to separate us from the love of God in Christ Jesus our Lord. (Romans 8:28–39 ESV)

Jesus Was Victimized, but He Was not a Victim

Jesus was victimized, but he never took on the identity of a victim. He was ridiculed, slandered, betrayed, tortured, and hung on a cross to die, yet he never retaliated or blamed what was happening to him on his offenders. On the cross, Jesus said, "Father, forgive them, for they do not know what they are doing" (Luke 23:34 NIV). He knew what was going to happen to him, but he let it happen willingly without retaliation (John 10:15–18).

Jesus was not a victim for three reasons. First, he trusted his life to his heavenly Father. His security was in his identity as the Son of God. How could the Son of God see himself as a victim? In like manner, our identity is in Jesus. Two, he made himself vulnerable to man out of obedience to his heavenly Father. In other words, he was more concerned about his Father's will and purposes than his own. We can do the same. We can live victoriously in this sinful world by trusting our lives to God for his service. Third, he loved his perpetrators. He looked with compassion on those who were hurting him. Jesus commands us to love our enemies (Matthew 5:43–48). If we want to be victorious, in humility we need to consider others before ourselves. Love is like a shield against a bitter and unforgiving heart, even when under the attack of those who dislike us.

If we are to escape an identity of being a victim, we must do as Jesus did. We must see ourselves as belonging to God. We must live our lives as servants of God for his purposes. God's servants are not victims; they are conquerors, fighting for the kingdom of God in this dark world. The day will come when we will inherit this marvelous kingdom.

If it is God's will for us to suffer, we are not victims. God loves us and he is using our lives for his purposes. Look at this account of the man born blind.

> As He was passing by, He saw a man blind from birth. His disciples questioned Him: "Rabbi, who sinned, this man or his parents, that he was born blind?"
>
> "Neither this man nor his parents sinned," Jesus answered. "[This came about] so that God's works might be displayed in him. We must do the works of Him who sent Me while it is day. Night is coming when no one can work. As long as I am in the world, I am the light of the world."
>
> After He said these things He spit on the ground, made some mud from the saliva, and spread the mud on his eyes. "Go," He

told him, "wash in the pool of Siloam" (which means "Sent"). So he left, washed, and came back seeing. (John 9:1–7 HCSB)

After this man was healed, he was used as powerful testimony that served to witness Jesus as coming from God. This man was not a victim. He was created by God as a testimony for God. He was born blind, but not as a curse or because of sin. He was born blind so that the glory of God could be revealed in his life. If we are children of God, we are loved by God. And anything that happens in our lives can be used by God to bring him glory. This glory begins with our attitude. A victim attitude does not bring about his glory. Praise for God, thanks to God, faith in God, faithfulness to God, trust in God, obedience to God, and love for God do bring about his glory. That is how Jesus brought glory to God upon this earth. Jesus suffered at the hands of humans, but Jesus was definitely not a victim.

Our daughter Abigail was diagnosed with leukemia when she was ten years old. She was on chemotherapy for two and a half years. She is fine today at twenty-one, but at the time we did not know if she would live. I asked God why he allowed this to happen. In those first weeks the love from the body of Christ poured out upon us. People prayed, they called, and they brought over meals and gifts. Then the Lord revealed to me why. My daughter had cancer in her body, but Jesus' body has the spiritual cancer of sin. Through my daughter's illness, Jesus' body was being healed as they poured out their love for us. When we love, sin is gone.

Affirmation from Jesus

We all need to be affirmed, and most of us struggle for affirmation. Affirmation defines who we are in the eyes of someone else. Victims typically do not feel affirmed by others or by God. Jesus did not look to the people for his affirmation; he looked to his heavenly Father. He was continuously about his Father's work here on earth (John 4:34; 5:17, 36; 9:4; 17:4). His affirmation was all about pleasing his Father in heaven. We all desire to be affirmed by others, but our first source of affirmation needs to come from Jesus, as we are about his work upon this earth in our individual lives. Those who have served Jesus will hear from him the words we all strive to hear.

His master said to him, "Well done, good and faithful servant. You have been faithful over a little; I will set you over much. Enter into the joy of your master." (Matthew 25:21 ESV)

Jesus commands us to love one another—whether we are loved in return, affirmed in return, or not (John 15:12–19; Matthew 25:31–46). Victims are forever seeking affirmation and are never victorious. Their self-imposed victim status says, "Look at me; I am a victim. Notice me!" Seeking affirmation from others for personal security and identity will always leave you short and frustrated. The lack of affirmation may even cause you to feel more like a victim. Victory comes from serving Jesus and looking to him for affirmation. Jesus does not let us down. His work in us is eternal, and so is his affirmation. Jesus calls those who obey his command to love his friends and partners in what he is doing in his business. (John 15:9–17). As Christ-followers, we work for the Creator, the King of Kings. What greater identity! What greater affirmation!

Focus on What Jesus Is Doing in Us

Victims focus on the past, what others have done to them. Victims focus on the present, how they are being victimized by others. Victims do not live in the joy of becoming like Jesus as his Spirit works in our lives. Victims do not live in the great hope of a glorious future in the kingdom of God.

God is the one who will avenge our enemies. He is the one who will raise us up. He is the one who will reward us in the end for doing his will and for glorifying his name. As children of God, we are to keep our eyes on Jesus' victory in our lives. A day is coming when all of our enemies will be destroyed. Those who belong to Jesus will rise to reign with him in his kingdom forever. The battles of this life will be over, and we will never have anything to fear again. God is working in us to transform us and to make us strong in character and faith. This is our hope, and this hope will not disappoint us.

> We have also obtained access through Him by faith into this grace in which we stand, and we rejoice in the hope of the glory of God. And not only that, but we also rejoice in our afflictions, because we know that affliction produces endurance, endurance produces proven character, and proven character produces hope. This hope will not disappoint [us], because God's love has been poured out in our hearts through the Holy Spirit who was given to us. (Romans 5:2–5 HCSB)

Having the right perspective produces the right attitude. We may suffer now, but God will use our suffering to mold and shape us. He may even use our suffering to bring about his purposes and glory. We wait patiently in our suffering, not viewing ourselves as victims, for we set our hope on the glorious day when we will be delivered and revealed as the sons of the living God.

> The Spirit Himself testifies together with our spirit that we are God's children, and if children, also heirs—heirs of God and coheirs with Christ—seeing that we suffer with Him so that we may also be glorified with Him.
>
> For I consider that the sufferings of this present time are not worth comparing with the glory that is going to be revealed to us. For the creation eagerly waits with anticipation for God's sons to be revealed. For the creation was subjected to futility—not willingly, but because of Him who subjected it—in the hope that the creation itself will also be set free from the bondage of corruption into the glorious freedom of God's children. For we know that the whole creation has been groaning together with labor pains until now. And not only that, but we ourselves who have the Spirit as the firstfruits—we also groan within ourselves, eagerly waiting for adoption, the redemption of our bodies. Now in this hope we were saved, yet hope that is seen is not hope, because who hopes for what he sees? But if we hope for what we do not see, we eagerly wait for it with patience. (Romans 8:16–25 HCSB)

Forgiving Those Who Harmed Us

Many who maintain a victim identity at one time were truly victims. In order to take on a new identity, it is imperative to forgive those who abused us in the past, or maybe even in the present. *Forgiveness is the power to become victorious.*

Jesus was victorious on the cross when he asked his Father to forgive those who mocked him and hung him on the cross (Luke 23:34). Our victory will not come without forgiving those who offended us. Forgiveness brings freedom and power. Unforgiveness keeps us in bondage. Unforgiveness eats away at the inside. It separates us from others. Unforgiveness is bitter. It makes us a true victim. Forgiveness is true victory. Forgiveness releases us so that we can love. Forgiveness is love.

God is love. As his children with his Spirit living within us, we are to love sacrificially. Love is victorious. The love of Christ for us as he hung on the cross defeated the Devil. Our love for others will bring us victory over all enemies. We do not have to be victims. We can be victorious. Walking in the character of Christ is the secret to victory.

> Do not repay anyone evil for evil. Try to do what is honorable in everyone's eyes. If possible, on your part, live at peace with everyone. Friends, do not avenge yourselves; instead, leave room for His wrath. For it is written: Vengeance belongs to Me; I will repay, says the Lord. But if your enemy is hungry, feed him. If he is thirsty, give him something to drink. For in so doing you will be heaping fiery coals on his head. Do not be conquered by evil, but conquer evil with good. (Romans 12:17–21 HCSB)

Retaliation and vengeance do not bring about victory; they only increase the conflict and define us as victims. Love is our weapon against becoming a victim. Love never fails to raise up God. When we love, we are raised up in the eyes of God. Love diffuses our enemies, and it may even unite us with those who oppose us. Love is the power of God working in and through us. Love is always victorious.

The key is to recognize where you have viewed yourself as a victim and acted as a victim. Confess this to others, and repent of this destructive and possibly sinful way of living. Jesus desires to lead you out of captivity. He came so that you could be delivered from a victim identity and become a victorious child of God. Your identity may have been hidden in your past, but now it is to be hidden in Christ, who died for you and is your life.

> Therefore, if you have been raised with Christ, keep seeking the things above, where Christ is, seated at the right hand of God. Keep thinking about things above, not things on the earth, for you have died and your life is hidden with Christ in God. When Christ (who is your life) appears, then you too will be revealed in glory with him. (Colossians 3:1–4 NET)

Reflection Questions

How have you viewed yourself as a victim? How have you acted out a victim role? (Quickly review each chapter to recall what you have learned about yourself.)

How should you view yourself? What can make you victorious in the face of pain, obstacles, situations, attacks, rejections, or any adverse circumstances? Describe the change in attitude required (before versus after). What does repentance look like?

Are you willing to confess your view as a victim to others and choose to repent so that you can walk victoriously?

What will it cost you personally to come out of the victim role? Where will you need courage? Where will you have to give up your old selfish ways of behaving?

How might you act in love toward those who once were perceived as your enemies? Who do you need to forgive and for what?

How is the role of a victim opposite from being a child of God? How is being a child of God a place of victory? Where does your affirmation come from?